The
Power
of Your
Senses

The
Power
of Your
Senses

**Why Coffee Tastes Better in a Red Cup
and Other Life-Changing Science**

RUSSELL JONES

WELBECK

Published by Welbeck
An imprint of Welbeck Non-Fiction Limited,
part of Welbeck Publishing Group.
20 Mortimer Street,
London W1T 3JW

First published by Welbeck in 2020

A CIP catalogue record for this book is available from the British Library

ISBN
Paperback - 9781787395046
eBook - 9781787395657

Typeset by EnvyDesign
Printed and bound by CPI Group (UK) Ltd., Croydon, CR0 4YY

10 9 8 7 6 5 4 3 2 1

www.welbeckpublishing.com

For Linus

Contents

Introduction   1

    The Provençal Rosé Paradox   1

    We're Feeling Machines   8

    The Synaesthetic Mind   11

    Sensory Prescriptions   16

1. The Morning   21

    Waking Up   22

        A Sensory Prescription for a Multisensory   28
        Alarm Clock

    Getting Dressed – Enclothed Cognition   30

    A Spritz of Fragrance   34

    Breakfast   39

        How to Encourage Healthy Choices   42

        How to Increase Sweetness and Indulgence 46

2. Sight   47

3. Exercise   57

  Getting Ready   59

    A Sensory Prescription for Pre-Workout Prep   64

  Working Out   64

    A Sensory Prescription for a Better Workout   74

  Recovery   75

    A Sensory Prescription for Your Post-   78
    Workout Recovery

4. Sound   79

5. Work   87

  Where to Work – Your Immediate Environment   88

  First Thing – Being Productive   95

    A Sensory Prescription for Productivity, Focus   103
    and Attention to Detail

  Mid-Morning – Selling Yourself and Your Ideas   103

    A Sensory Prescription for Confidence,   118
    Competence and Getting Others to Say 'Yes'

  Lunchtime – The Power of Planning a Treat   119
  for Later

  Early Afternoon – Better Collaboration and   121
  Teamwork

    A Sensory Prescription for Social Interaction,   128
    Conversation and Working Together

  Mid-Afternoon – Being Creative   130

    A Sensory Prescription for Creativity and   139
    Creative Thinking

  Late Afternoon – Speeding Up time   139

A Sensory Prescription to Speed Up Time   143

6. Touch   145

7. Shopping   153
Making Healthier Choices   153
Sensory Influences in the Shopping   155
Environment: Sight, Touch, Smell, Taste
and Sound.

8. Smell   171

9. Home   179
The Coming-Home Ritual   180
    A Sensory Prescription for a Coming-Home   188
    Ritual
The Emotions and Functions of Each Room   189
Scenting Your Home – An Emotional Journey   192
of Discovery
Slowing Down Time   200
    A Sensory Prescription to Slow Down Time   203
Immersive Cinema (Or a Box Set) at Home   204
Sensory Travel Planning   208

10. Taste   211

11. Dinner and Drinks   219
Preparing the Meal – Some Considerations   221
    Cutlery   222

Artistic Presentation 222

Guest Involvement 222

A Wine-List Playlist – Matching Music
to Wine 225

A Sensorial Dinner Party 229

Aroma Mixology – A Sensory Cocktail Tasting 229
Experiment

Starter 232

Main Course 234

The Between-Course Tongue Twister – 235
A Colour and Taste Challenge

Dessert 237

Digestif 241

12. The Other Senses 245

13. Sex 253

The Build-Up 255

During Sex 262

A Sensory Prescription for Better Sex 270

The Afterglow – Ready to Go Again 270

14. Sleep 275

A Countdown to Bed 277

A Sensory Prescription for Better Sleep 286

While You Are Sleeping 287

Acknowledgements 293

Introduction

The Provençal Rosé Paradox

Imagine yourself on holiday in the South of France. You're sitting on the terrace of an old auberge that you have happened by for lunch, eating steak frites. Rolling fields of lavender disappear off into the distance. Around you the gentle murmur of French voices and the clinking of cutlery and wine glasses creates a calm and distinctly Mediterranean backdrop to this picture-perfect scene. The sun is warm; you feel relaxed and at ease. A waiter brings out an earthenware carafe of beautifully chilled rosé. It's delicious; pale rose gold; the perfect accompaniment to the moment, the location and the vista. You ask him where this wonderful drop is from, and he tells you that it's from a vineyard just down the road. You stop there on your way back to the villa, and to your amazement the wine only costs two euros a bottle. You buy tons of it and drink it happily all holiday – and of course, you also bring a case back home with you.

Now it's February. You're drowning once more in the daily grind and drudgery of life. Outside, the relentless darkness and freezing rain have been driving you to despair now for some weeks. Work is getting you down again as usual. However, tonight is a treat as you have invited some old friends over for dinner. Talk turns to your wonderful holiday in Provence the previous summer and you tell tale of the beautiful local rosé you found. Only two euros a bottle! And delicious; you have some in the fridge. Your guests emit pleasing moans of expectation, commenting on the wonderful colour as you pour them a glass.

You sip; it's disgusting, vinegary and acidic. Truly cheap plonk. 'It's gone bad!' you exclaim. Such a shame – it must have got ruined in the back of the car on the drive home, bouncing up and down on those French country roads; and in the heat too. But no, you have fallen prey to the 'Provençal rosé paradox'. The wine is the same as it always was; what has changed is everything else. You're no longer feeling relaxed, basking in the warm glow of the afternoon Provençal sun. You're not surrounded by the sounds, smells and colours that helped create the experience where you formed that wonderful memory; it was the environment and your emotional state that conspired to alter your perception and make the wine taste so good.

But all is not lost – we can bring the taste back by setting up a sensory scene that is evocative of that moment. Maybe you could light a lavender-scented candle for the distant aroma. Decant the wine into an earthenware carafe. Lay the table with a red and white chequered tablecloth. Put on some Edith Piaf records or the hubbub of French chatter. Recreate the sensory environment, recall the memories and evoke the same emotions, and the wine will be pleasing on the palate once more. Perhaps not quite as thirst-quenchingly, soul-inspiringly delicious as it was at that auberge in France, but much better than the plonk that you're tasting now.

For the last ten years or so, I've been telling that story as an introduction in boardroom presentations, as a way of illustrating how our perception is influenced by everything around us. To show that our senses and emotions cross over, affecting our experience of the world. That one sense, which we believe works completely on its own and is always telling you the truth – in this case taste – is in actual fact the product of multiple triggers and stimuli we're picking up through every other sense at the same time; and coloured further by our emotional state. We are multisensory beings, but we tend to exist and think one sense at a time. This is not how it works.

Research from the worlds of neuroscience, experimental psychology and behavioural psychology has uncovered the amazing extent to which our behaviour and perception are affected by what seem like arbitrary factors in our environment. Like the fact that coffee tastes sweeter if you drink it from a red and rounded mug. Or that we perceive time to pass by more quickly when we are in a blue room with slow music playing. Smells that remind us of the past encourage us to seek out new ideas. We buy more indulgent products when we're cold. Food tastes 11 per cent more delicious when it's eaten using heavy cutlery. And white wine tastes 15 per cent more zingy if you listen to Blondie while drinking it. I've been applying this area of sensory study in my work for a while now – discovering neuroscientific insights into how our senses and emotions interact, and using them to design better products, brands, spaces and experiences, in a scientifically proven way.

Here's a good example: my agency was approached by a global ice cream brand who wanted to claim that their cone possessed the quintessential crunch. It was our job to define the key components that deliver the sensation and provide their development team with direction. The process we go through is similar, regardless of the project: first we conduct a literature review, looking at existing research that might give us guidance on where to go. It turned out that a scientist called Zata Vickers thoroughly investigated crunchiness between the late 1970s and the early 1990s. Her research argues that it is almost entirely down to what you hear – if something doesn't *sound* crunchy, it isn't crunchy. She and her team also suggested that the ultimate crunch is within a range of sonic pitch, above which a sound becomes crispy. Based on this, we started to test some ideas. We recorded biting into the client's cone and made versions of the sound at different pitches. We then ran an online study in which we asked people to listen to the sounds and judge how crunchy they thought the cones were, and how much they liked the idea of eating one. The client's current cone was too high-pitched and decidedly crispy; a slightly lower-pitched version was judged to be the crunchiest of all, and that was the one that people most fancied eating. We had pinpointed 'the ultimate crunch'. Next we visited Professor Barry Smith, director of University of London's Centre for the Study of the Senses, and set up an experiment. We had people eating ice creams in front of microphones, with the sound being fed through a computer and back to headphones that our participants were wearing. We were able to control what they heard as they ate the ice creams in real time. When we made the sound high-pitched, the cones tasted light and crispy. By muffling the sound, we could make them seem stale. And by pushing the sound into the 'ultimate crunch' range, the cones tasted crunchy and were more enjoyable to eat. The ice cream itself also tasted richer and creamier, due to what is called a 'halo effect'; when one sense is pleased, the others often follow suit.

With these results, we had a brief for a new cone. The development scientists went back to the lab and created one that made the exact sound when bitten into. Armed with this new product, we ran consumer testing again; people said it was crunchier, creamier and better quality, and judged that they would pay 20p more for it. The only thing that had changed was the sound made when the cone was bitten.

My approach considers the entire sensory experience

of buying and eating a product, so we didn't stop there. We looked at the language used when describing it in adverts and on the packaging: how the words used can prime expectations of how the product will taste – sharp and staccato sounds cut to the crunch, while creamy words flow slowly and smooth. We explored different textures on the packaging to make it feel and sound crunchy as you tear it open, making you expect the ultimate crunch even before you tuck in. We looked at the action of unwrapping the product – could the movements you make enhance the taste in some way? A swirling motion would feel creamy, while the sound would be crunchy. We also created a crunchy 'sonic mnemonic' (the sound that accompanies the logo and product shot at the end of an advert) and selected music that contained crunchy guitars and a staccato rhythm. In this way, from the moment of seeing and hearing the advert, picking up and unwrapping the product, a consumer would be led on a sensory journey that would build expectation and finally deliver a crunchy experience from the first bite.

Now, some people may see this approach as a manipulation – 'You didn't actually improve the taste!' they might protest. 'Aren't people being fooled into believing it's better?' Well, the point is, it *is* better. We improved the taste and made the ice cream more enjoyable, but we did it by looking at how humans experience the world through every sense, all at the same time.

We live every moment of our lives in this multisensory

way, though most of us don't realise it. I passionately believe that if we did, every experience would become richer. The sensory science is there to improve exercise, sleep, work, food and sex, but there's an art to applying it to our lives: knowing which sounds, smells, colours and textures go together to elicit a certain response. It's something I've been doing for a long time, for everything from ice cream, whisky and beer, to luxury cars and department stores.

With corporate budgets behind me and defined outcomes to achieve, I found a way to take the academic study and explore its practical application, using the science to affect and enhance real-world situations. Influencing behaviour and perception through the smallest change in the sensory environment; whether the goal was to encourage people to talk to staff in a shop or to make a whisky taste sweeter and richer. I have built a career and somewhat invented an industry, approaching the design of everything we do from a multisensory point of view. In this book, I will show you how you can do this in your own life, living more multisensorially while understanding the science and being aware of your senses. Once you do, you will find yourself stepping into a brighter and bolder place, like Dorothy walking out into technicolour Oz.

Before we begin a multisensory journey through the day, let's explore how our senses influence us so profoundly. It works on two levels: one that involves emotions and memories, like the Provençal rosé paradox, and another that involves deep-rooted 'cross-modal' links. In reality they aren't so separate, but I think this idea sets up the world we're about to enter well enough. Firstly, then, let us venture further into our memories and emotions.

We're Feeling Machines

'We are not thinking machines that feel; we are feeling machines that think.' This fantastic quote is by Professor Antonio Damasio, from his book *Descartes' Error: Emotion, Reason and the Human Brain*. It encapsulates why our senses are so influential over our actions; we might think that we're rational beings that make well-thought-out, intelligent decisions, but we're not. We're emotional machines; we make emotional decisions and then post-rationalise them. And the way to influence the emotions is through the senses.

Buying a house is a classic example. You might begin your search armed with a list of sensible criteria: that it has to be within a certain distance from schools and the train station, or that it needs a spare room for the home office. Then, on walking into 'the one', everything goes out of the window. You get a feeling, and instantly know that this has *got* to be your home. Something intangible caused a rush of endorphins that made you feel 'this is the place'. You could call it some kind of extrasensory perception, but it's more a moment of 'multisensory perception', a combination of elements that came together to trigger feelings that represent what 'home' or 'family' means to you. It might be an evocative smell, or the way warm daylight filled the room. The soft, dampened sound that made the space feel welcoming. Pictures or decorations that primed thoughts of happy families and lasting love. Some kind of sensorial harmony throughout the place, with all these elements combining to bring these feelings to the front of your mind. You convince yourself for your newly adjusted emotional standpoint with rational arguments. There isn't a spare room, but you can build an office at the end of the garden; it'll be nice to have a working space that is separate from the house, anyway. And actually, being so far away from the station is fine, because getting there every morning will be good exercise.

As we go through life experiencing the world and forging memories, we learn to associate different feelings with the sensory elements around us. For example, the smell of sun cream makes us feel happy, because we're always happy when we use it. Or the colour green reminds us of nature and is connected with notions of healthiness. These smells, colours and sounds become triggers for their associated feelings and meanings, and it's always the emotion that comes first, before you are able to acknowledge where the memory is from or what sparked it.

Think about a time when you came across a piece of music that you listened to a lot as a kid; the feeling of that time comes rushing back immediately, then you start kicking yourself as you try to remember who it's by. When these emotions or connections rise to the surface, they become accessible to our decision-making brain, and it becomes more likely that your thinking process and behaviours will go that way when faced with a choice. An old adage for this is 'the rider and the elephant'. The rider is the rational part of the brain – the prefrontal cortex – and the elephant is your emotional brain – the limbic system, to which the senses, especially sound and scent, are the superhighway. If the elephant catches wind of something that sparks its interest, then off it will go, and the rider can't do a thing about it. Maybe a scent in the air reminded it of being a calf, exploring the jungle to its heart's content. Nostalgic feelings of adventure and curiosity rise to the surface of its mind, and all the rider can do is go along for the ride. If we understand what emotions motivate the elephant and which sensory stimuli will spark certain thought processes or behaviours, the rider can take back control.

For instance, researchers in New Zealand looked at how different sensory stimuli in a shopping environment can influence our choices when it comes to buying healthy or unhealthy food. Participants were asked to peruse a 'virtual supermarket' on computers and buy three days' worth of shopping. Different groups completed the task while the smell of either fresh herbs or sweet baking was wafted into the air, at a level that wasn't particularly noticeable (only 5 per cent of the participants acknowledged the smell). The people in the herb-scented group tended to choose healthier items and bought more wholefoods than the group who were exposed to the baking smell. The subtle background scent primed notions of freshness, green herbs and nature, which bubbled up to the surface of the subjects' minds, making them reach for the healthier products.

So how can we use this emotional reaction to our own advantage? How can we control the elephant? Our choice of sensory stimuli triggers memories and emotions that directly influence our actions and perception. So we must try to ensure that every component in an environment works together towards a desired outcome, whether that's affecting a behaviour, helping you think a certain way, or improving your enjoyment of a glass of rosé.

The Synaesthetic Mind

There is another level to our sensory experience of the world, which reveals a crossing of the senses that goes right to the core of our being: the synaesthetic mind. This refers to the fact that we all link one sensory quality with another. To begin exploring this cross-sensory world I'll pose a simple question, which I would like you to answer without thinking: is the taste of a lemon fast or slow?

What's the first thing that comes to mind? Virtually everyone says that lemons taste fast. I've asked the question to a room of 200 people and they've all shouted out 'fast' in unison. When I ask people to give me a reason, they sometimes offer quite rational, or at least understandable, answers: 'Because the taste hits you instantly.' 'Because they're zingy.' Or I've heard explanations that drift into the bizarre: 'Because they're shaped like a torpedo.' 'Because they're yellow, and so are sports cars.' The point is that none of the answers make sense, but they all reveal our strange but instinctual crossing of the senses.

Here's another version. Look at the two shapes below – one is spiky and the other is round and globular. Which of them is the taste of a lemon?

I'm hopeful that I can predict your answer. The taste of a lemon is sharp and angular. If I were to ask which of the two shapes is milk chocolate, which would you say? Which one is more refreshing? Which is more active?

It's fascinating that we can plot pretty much all tastes, flavours, sensations and feelings on a scale between these two shapes. And we can go further, to texture, weight, colour and pitch. These instinctual links between a characteristic we experience through one sense and a quality we attribute to another reveal an extra dimension of the human experience that we're not even aware of – but it's always there, shaping and colouring our perception and our behaviour. And we all seem to be on the same page when it comes to what goes with what. Regardless of where they are in the world, people will more than likely agree that the taste of a lemon is fast and sharp, high-pitched and brightly coloured.

What is happening, to some extent, can be described as a low-level form of synaesthesia, or 'joined perception'. Full-on synacsthesia affects around 1 in 250 of the population. A person with the condition will experience two or more senses together in a completely real way. Some might see cascading colours when they hear music. Or they might hear musical tones when they look at different colours or combinations of colour. Some synaesthetic people say a word and experience flavours on their tongue, as if they are actually tasting something. In a book called *The Frog Who Croaked Blue*, Jamie Ward writes about a man who tasted strawberries whenever he said 'Paris' and condensed milk when he said 'teddy bear'. He was asked if he could taste strawberries and cream when he said 'Paris teddy bear', but he tried it and tasted something completely different and quite acrid.

A lot of creative people, especially artists and musicians, have been known to be synaesthetic, perhaps due to the unique view of the world the condition gives you. The Russian painter Wassily Kandinsky famously heard music when he saw colours and saw colours when he heard music. It is said that he decided to dedicate himself to painting after a particularly powerful synaesthetic experience at a performance of Wagner's *Lohengrin*. He later described the life-changing moment: 'I saw all my colours in spirit, before my eyes. Wild, almost crazy lines were sketched in front of me.' Duke Ellington and Leonard Bernstein similarly saw colours when they played, listened to or composed music. Bernstein described how he chose the textures and timbres of sounds available in an orchestra as if from a palette of colours, with each finished piece a balanced landscape of shades and 'musical colours'. Marilyn Monroe was also reported to have chromesthesia, the form of synaesthesia where music and colours collide. Norman Mailer wrote about her that 'She has that displacement of the senses which others take drugs to find.' Vladimir Nabokov had grapheme-colour synaesthesia – when sounding out letters, he experienced colours. In the 'blue group', he said, there was 'steely x, thundercloud z and huckleberry k … I see q as browner than k, while s is not the light blue of c, but a curious mixture of azure and mother-of-pearl.' The list of creative synaesthetes goes on, from Billy Joel to the actor Geoffrey Rush, Vincent van Gogh to Mary J. Blige and, apparently, Kanye West.

As to why or how we have this jumbling up of the senses, there doesn't seem to be a concrete answer. One argument is that they are learned through our interactions with the world around us and derived from the language we use. We see fruit that tastes sweeter when it is rich red, so the colour sways our perception to pick up its sweetness rather than other flavours. We talk about 'loud colours', 'sharp tastes' and 'sweet music' – have these terms trained us to make these sensory connections, or have they evolved to represent sensory links that are part of our being? Researchers in Germany identified similar cross-sensory connections in chimpanzees, showing that they related high-pitched sounds to white squares and low-pitched sound to black squares, just like we do. The scientists argued that the chimps could not have learned the link between musical pitch and colour brightness through their ecological environment; it proves, they said, that these sensory correspondences must be inherent and have formed before our ancient ancestors split in their evolutionary path.

The important point is that these connections undeniably exist in all of us. And as we will go on to explore, if we use the cross-sensory connections that we all have in one 'synaesthetic experience', they can feed off each other and deliver a heightened effect – referred to as a 'super-additive' effect. Drink a lemon-flavoured drink from a glass with an angular shape, and you will perceive the lemon taste to be more zingy and sharp. You will feel more active and think sharper in a room filled with angular objects and a sharp, zesty scent than you would in a room with curved furniture and a warm sweet aroma.

I am adept at taking all these different components and bringing them together, and this is what I will try to impart to you in this book. I identify cross-sensory associations, and the effects memories and emotions have on our behaviour and perception, while also looking at the physiological impact that colours, light, sounds and smells have on us. We can even look at our own natural cycle throughout the day and identify when we're more receptive to certain behaviours and ideas. I will pull all this together to create what I call a 'sensory prescription' that details what every sensory ingredient should be to deliver the ideal environment for what you want to do, feel or experience.

Sensory Prescriptions

When I started writing this book, I was working on a project for John Lewis, the British department store and high street institution. My business partner Jo and I were helping to design a space within the home furnishings department of each store where customers could decide on an interior scheme, choosing the colour palette, materials, furniture, lighting and decoration. The space needed to encourage a sense of play in the customers, bringing out their creativity. They also needed to feel comfortable to pick things up, touching the products and material swatches, as well as spending time talking to staff and interacting with the environment. We Brits are traditionally quite reserved in how we shop, acting like we are in some kind of art gallery where one shouldn't touch anything and must always speak in hushed tones.

Jo and I began our process as we always do: we tried to uncover the sensory elements that encourage the behaviours and elicit the feelings that would help this space deliver its purpose. Nostalgic, 'experience-based' aromas, like the smell of freshly cut grass, encourage 'approach-motivated behaviours', which means we are more likely to explore new things and ideas. We are less inhibited and more creative under higher ceilings and lower lighting. A sense of playfulness is intrinsically linked with brighter colours, while complex, abstract imagery makes us more playful than minimalist designs or literal pictures. Soft textures and warm materials encourage collaboration. There's an optimal level of noise that causes a beneficial level of mental distraction, where creativity creeps in. Too loud and it is intrusive; too quiet and we feel self-conscious. All these insights come together to form a set of sensorial guidelines for creativity, exploration and collaboration. This 'sensory prescription' was then handed to the designers with whom we were working. When it came together, the introduction of bright, abstract art, low lighting, soft materials, nostalgic aromas and a low-level of background sound and music provided an environment that enabled shoppers to break free of their inherent British politeness and let their creative juices flow. There's a lot more about these insights and the research behind them later in the book!

The term 'sensory prescription' came about because of the idea that, just as a doctor would prescribe a combination of pills, diet, rest and mild activity (though sadly, mostly just pills), we can prescribe an environment of sounds, colours and smells to help with a specific problem. The term is even more appropriate when you look at the genuine benefits that it can have in the realm of medical care – the effects can be psychological *and* physiological. A trial was conducted in a Swedish hospital in the mid-1990s: patients recovering from heart surgery were taken to a ward filled with the smell of vanilla, which has a naturally calming effect. This scent was coupled with coloured lighting in a hue called 'Baker-Miller pink' – proven to reduce stress and aggression; it's used by the military to calm down rowdy incarcerated soldiers. A soundtrack of tumbling waves, which lowers the heart rate and stress levels, completed the atmosphere.

The positive effects of the experiment were significant. It resulted in patients needing less pain medication, reduced their levels of stress and led to them being discharged earlier. Hospitals are generally sensorially quite unforgiving, so it beggars belief why this approach isn't rolled out globally. More thought should be given to how the body and mind can be nourished in hospitals, rather than the sole focus being on how they can be functional for medical practice.

I picture a day when the idea of sensory prescription could be used in hospitals. Patients might be handed a card reminiscent of a hotel room key that, on being inserted into a slot by their door (or their 'wellness pod' maybe!) would switch the lights to a specific colour and brightness, as well as triggering a soundtrack and an aroma diffuser. All this would be designed to assist the patient's recovery from their specific ailment. It is perfectly feasible, and the research shows how effective getting the right sensory prescription can be. Until then, we have our own homes, offices and general life to take care of, so that's where we need to start.

INTRODUCTION

I've structured this book around a typical day, in order to cover as many activities that we might encounter in our lives as possible. From waking up, breakfasting and exercising, to being productive and more creative at work. And from setting up a multisensory home to having super sensory meals, better sex and getting a good night's sleep.

I've always believed that we should be more sensorially aware, and have always enjoyed imparting this knowledge. When people ask me what I do, I tend to find that they are fascinated when I tell them about it. It comes as a revelation, but also makes perfect sense and feels instinctually right. Now, by focusing my insight and experience onto every aspect of a daily routine, I hope I've found a way that people can apply my knowledge to their lives in a practical way.

To accompany many of the moments throughout the day, I've created sounds, music playlists and films that can be accessed through the *Sense* website.

There is a lot of information within these pages; by using just a fraction of the tips and insights, every moment of your day can be changed for the better. No longer will you drink wine while listening to entirely incongruent music, or try to brainstorm at a tidy desk while sitting under a bright light; you will possess the knowledge and ability to make your world a more sensorially stimulating and harmonious place. I hope you use it well.

CHAPTER 1

The Morning

We will assume this day begins as most days should, with you waking from restful sleep in your own bed. By the time you've finished this book, if you practise some of the lessons in it, your night should have been peaceful, with your body clock appropriately aligned to the cycle of day and night.

Dwelling on that for a moment, from time to time in this book there will be references to our internal body clock and the 'circadian rhythm', so I should quickly summarise that very important topic. The circadian rhythm is a twenty-four-hour cycle of biological processes that's present in virtually every living thing, from microbes and fungi to humans. It is a predictable pattern of functions such as hormone production, cell regeneration and brain wave activity that are involved in regulating things like our sleep, moods and cognitive performance. An internal clock controlled by a small area in the middle of the brain called the suprachiasmatic nucleus, it resets itself every day according to the earth's rotation.

Despite this astronomical connection, the circadian rhythm is also affected by some localised external and environmental factors called 'zeitgebers', a term literally meaning 'time-givers' coined by Jürgen Aschoff, the German physiologist and father of chronobiology. These zeitgeber can be things like light or temperature, or even changes in your emotional state throughout the day. And so, coming from a multisensory point of view, your surroundings play a very important part in keeping your rhythm in time, aligning your biological clock with your daily routine so that at the end of the day you can get a good night's sleep, and wake up feeling as rested and raring to go as possible.

Waking Up

In our quest for the best wake-up, we need a multisensory approach that will draw you out of slumber and start your clock for the day. The senses that are most in play while you're sleeping are sight and hearing – scent, which you may assume is always present, is missing from the line-up at this point. Research has shown that aromas are registered in the brain during sleep, but not nearly enough to rouse you from slumber. The question is, what are the ideal sights and sounds to wake up to?

SOFT LIGHT

In terms of our circadian rhythm, the best possible wake-up system is light, the number one 'zeitgeber'. It is evolutionarily ingrained in us to be awake, cognitive and energetic in daylight and to rest and recuperate at night. If it were possible to wake up under a beautiful blue sky every morning, we would be in a much better position. A study at a sleep laboratory in Colorado took a group camping in the Rockies and measured their circadian rhythms and levels of melatonin, the sleep hormone. Back in their electric-light-filled homes, they not only woke up later, but their morning 'melatonin onset', a burst of the hormone that is meant to happen while asleep, was kicking in about two hours after they got up, causing them to be groggy for the first few hours of the day – a condition called 'sleep inertia' that can affect people to quite severe levels. While they were camping, the participants slept and rose two hours earlier than they would usually, so their morning melatonin burst occurred about an hour before they woke, right on time. Exposure to longer periods of natural light had brought their hormones and sleep patterns together, aligning their circadian rhythms and body clocks.

As far as our normal daily lives are concerned, we can't always camp under the stars (and many people don't want to). Leaving the curtains open overnight isn't practical for most because of light pollution and the potential voyeurism of nosy neighbours. Nor do we all rise with the sun anyway, especially in the dark days of winter. We can, however, get close to the real thing with the help of a light-based alarm. Studies into the effects of 'artificial dawn' alarm clocks that simulate sunrise have shown very positive results. Researchers in the Netherlands tested light alarms with different intensities on people who were complaining of sleep inertia; the effect on their hormones was not quite as pronounced as with natural light, but their symptoms of sleep inertia were greatly reduced, and the subjects woke up feeling more positive and energised. Results have repeatedly been best when using bright blue-white lamps that pump out 6,500K of light, attempting to simulate daylight. However, one study by the same group in the Netherlands showed a positive effect with less bright and warmer light. The team measured the reaction times of sixteen women who woke up under different light conditions and found that there was more improvement when the light was set to a dimmer 2,700K – about the colour and brightness of a sixty-watt bulb. This is good news because the benefits of waking up raring to go can be outweighed by the unpleasantness of waking up in a room filled with bright fluorescent light. Like coming to in an operating theatre.

The best colour and level of light to wake up in, then, should be somewhat bright, but still soft and warm. If we consider learned associations and emotions, a soft, pinkish hue would cast more of a fresh and positive light on the day, evoking thoughts of spring blossom. Ultimately, though, there is no substitute for daylight when it comes to being in harmony with the day. With this in mind, spending time outside is absolutely necessary for a good night's sleep and to align your sleep-wake cycle. Try to spend at least two hours exposed to natural light throughout the day and you should experience the benefit; if you can't, light-based alarms do help alleviate sleep inertia and get you up in a brighter mood – especially if you pair it with the right soundscape.

GENTLE, NATURAL SOUNDS

The standard method of being suddenly woken by the Wagnerian screeching of an alarm clock, signalling severe urgency of some kind, is a rather unpleasant start to the new day. They say we are born with only two innate fears – falling and loud noises – in which case, the stimulation of an evolutionarily wired fight-or-flight mechanism first thing in the morning seems ill-advised – in fact, it could be downright dangerous. According to a paper by Dr William B. White, chief of the Division of Hypertension and Clinical Pharmacology at the University of Connecticut, our blood pressure can reduce by up to 30 per cent during sleep, before surging above normal levels when we wake up. What he terms the 'early morning blood pressure surge' can statistically increase the chance of cardiac arrest in the first few hours of the day. So shocking yourself out of sleep is not a good idea. Especially if it's a Monday! A study in Japan that measured the blood pressure of 175 people from a rural town outside Tokyo found that readings were highest on a Monday morning and lowest on a Sunday. This correlates with the fact that a statistically significant number of cardiovascular events happen on a Monday. Could they get any worse?

While we sleep, our hearing remains switched on. According to the renowned sleep scientist Charles Czeisler, even the slightest sounds during the night are registered by our resting minds, forcing us to transition into a lighter level of sleep. This is something that we can use to our advantage. Being woken in the middle of a dream or deep sleep leaves us groggy, so the best sonic alarm would lift us into lighter and lighter states, before awakening us gently. The sound should begin quietly, and gradually increase in volume to a comfortable level.

Being woken up by an artificial and impersonal beep misses an opportunity to expose yourself to something more emotionally meaningful first thing in the morning. We can use the power of sound to stir a favourable feeling and trigger deeply embedded associations. We might look to the circadian rhythm and its internal alignment with the break of day and the light of dawn; in order that there will be some evolutionarily learned link with the *sounds* of the morning too. The go-to soundscape would therefore be the gentle introduction of birdsong, a sound associated with freshness, nature and rebirth. Evoking those feelings should also help to lift your mood and mental state as you rise from a good night's rest. Following that thread, the use of other fresh, natural sounds could be employed. An arctic wind or crashing waves. Although, you might then wake up feeling freezing cold, or potentially wetting the bed. I think birdsong is the safest bet.

The perfect alarm might play out as a slow build of gentle birdsong and gentle voices, increasing in volume over twenty minutes to gradually transition you into lighter sleep states. Musical elements like the tinkling of chimes could add a positive feeling, with a bustle of activity continuing to build until it resolves with the distant sound of a bell – still pleasant but slightly louder, just to make sure you're up. This would be a far more civilised and sympathetic sonic wake-up that would pair perfectly with the light, align with your circadian rhythm and leave you feeling positively chirpy for the day ahead. It would be so good, in fact, that I've created it and called it the Rose Garden Alarm. It is on the *Sense* website if you'd like to try it.

Now, the birds are chirping and you can sense a glow in the room, but there's no need to open your eyes just yet. It is time to engage your senses for a little morning workout – a bit of mindfulness mixed with some ninja training to help you be multisensorial all day long.

SENSORY TRAINING

I remember coming across an exercise as a child (in a 'ninja training handbook' that I had got out of the library) that has really resonated with me in later life, becoming something that I try to employ whenever possible. It was all about training the senses, focusing on them every morning to assess the world around you before you open your eyes. It's a good thing to try, not just if you're striving to become a stealthy warrior; sense-training exercises are common in mindfulness, CBT and other forms of behavioural therapy. Engaging your senses is an effective way to bring yourself into the present moment.

While you lie in bed, try to sense what the weather is like outside. What distant sounds can you hear? What smells can you notice? What can you taste? How do the bedsheets feel, and where are your limbs? Are other people already up, either in the house or bustling about outdoors? Take a moment to get all your senses working, and you'll start the day feeling more focused and connected. Your assessments will improve over time, as you train your senses. Give it thirty seconds or so, and then it's time to get out of bed.

A SENSORY PRESCRIPTION FOR A MULTISENSORY ALARM CLOCK

The ultimate wake-up involves a coordinated crescendo of light and sound, scheduled to fade up gradually and starting around twenty minutes before you want to wake.

- **Light** – Mimic the brightening sky at dawn with a controllable light alarm. If you have control over the colour of your light, a slightly pink-white colour would be an agreeable alternative to the cold and clinical feel of dawn blue.

- **Sound** – Use birdsong as an alarm that fades up slowly. Backing up the light with an emotionally charged and sensorially congruent soundtrack will help to trigger feelings of refreshment and the birth of a new day.
- **Focus on your senses** – Lie still for a moment and bring all your senses into focus by sensing the world around you.

The sound and light alarm is possible; wake-up lights with sound options are readily available, and otherwise you can combine two systems. For instance, if you have programmable lights, set them to fade up in the morning and sync your smartphone alarm to the same time, setting it to play the Rose Garden Alarm. Both will work together, gently coaxing you to the lightest state of sleep and then waking you up, bright and fresh.

Once you are up, blue light and LEDs are welcome as they supress melatonin and stimulate cortisol, the stress hormone that gives you a quick burst of fight-or-flight energy; so feel free to check your email, social media or whatever you get up to on your smartphone – you know you want to. On average, we spend three and a half hours staring at our phones every day, and if there's a moment when it is actually good for you, it's first thing in the morning. It will help wake you up and get you mentally alert – although depending on what you're looking at, it might also stress you out!

Getting Dressed – Enclothed Cognition

What sort of day lies ahead will determine how you get dressed. We behave and think in accordance with what we're wearing, especially when it comes to uniforms or items of clothing that are associated with specific roles or behaviours. This is all down to a phenomenon called 'enclothed cognition'.

The term was coined by Hajo Adam and Adam Galinsky from Northwestern University; they showed in a 2011 study that people wearing a lab coat performed better at tasks that tested their attention than when they were not wearing the coat or when they were wearing it but had been told that it was an artist's smock. The lab coat is associated with expertise and precision, attention to detail, so wearing it influenced the participants' mental processes; they made half as many mistakes when wearing the coat as those who weren't.

A similar study was conducted by Professor Karen Pine from Hertfordshire University. Pine got students to sit for mental agility tests while they were wearing either a plain T-shirt, their normal clothes or a Superman T-shirt. The average scores were 64 per cent for the normal or plain T-shirt wearers, and 74 per cent for the people with the 'S' on their chests. Those in the Superman T-shirts also felt that they were physically stronger, more likeable and more superior to others on a social comparison scale.

The real experts at this are children, who will go the whole hog and dress up for any activity. My six-year-old son Linus will put on a hard hat and a utility belt to help me hang a picture, or his Robin Hood costume if we're going to the woods – it's a charming habit that we unnecessarily lose as we grow up. I'm not suggesting that we completely change our outfit every time we undergo an activity; it could just be one item that gives us a boost, like the Superman T-shirt.

It might be that a smaller detail in our clothes, like a hidden pattern or an accessory, can have a similar effect. A group of PhD students from the fashion department at the School of Applied Science at Istanbul University found details in the Islamic 'Rumi' patterns on garments worn by two sultans of the Ottoman Empire that they believe were embroidered in order to stimulate a certain mindset in the wearer. There were small inclusions that only the sultan would be aware of, such as passages from the Quran written in code, or particular words and phrases. The theory is that this would encourage the sultan to remain calm while facing the more challenging aspects of the sultan's daily duties. It represents an early sign of awareness of enclothed cognition and evidence that even the smallest things can work, if they have meaning to the wearer.

So, if you identify what you want to be good at today or how you'd like to behave, you can choose an outfit and an accessory that will be beneficial. For instance:

CONFIDENT

The classic 1980s power suit certainly gives you a confidence boost. Or you might choose to dress in black. An online retailer asked over 1,000 of its customers which colours they would associate with different emotional qualities; black came first for confidence, intelligence and sexiness. Red came second for confidence, but it was also strongly associated with arrogance.

Depending on what type of confidence you're after, you can choose an appropriate accessory. A skull necklace might help when you want to have attitude. Or you can choose something symbolic to you, like your father's watch to make you feel more grown up. (And yes, if my dad is reading this, that was a hint to give me his Rolex.)

CLERICAL

If you have a list of items to tick off or figures to crunch, dress as an office clerk: wear glasses and sensible clothes. For the ultimate impact on accuracy and attention to detail, you might choose to don a lab coat, if you have one to hand.

CREATIVE

Throw on a smock and a beret if you're planning to get your easel out and create a masterpiece. Or if you don't want to dress up, loosen your attire a little; less formal and restrictive clothes will promote less formal and restrictive thinking.

MEETING PEOPLE

If you're meeting lots of people, wear something that makes you feel open and warm to others. You might choose to put on something that you received as a gift, to remind you of the goodness inherent in other people.

HEALTHY

For an active day, put on your gym outfit. Dressing in garish spandex leggings and a sporty zip-up top will make you feel like you've done something good for yourself, even if you haven't actually made it to the gym. And you'll be less likely to binge on cake or have a burger for lunch if you do so.

INDULGENT

If you have a lazy day planned and want to be guilt-free, dressing in your schlumpy jogging bottoms and an old T-shirt will help reduce your brain to the required level of mush.

You can start to accumulate some of these mind-altering items of clothing as you go through life. If you buy yourself something after a moment of triumph, such as winning an important bit of work, you will from then on associate that item with that feeling. If you wear a particular piece of clothing every time you practise something creative like playing the piano, you can build up an association between it and your creative mindset. Whatever meaning you place on individual items can be used to your advantage, making yourself a better version of you – not just changing how you feel, but enhancing how you think.

A Spritz of Fragrance

Applying a splash of your favourite scent in the morning is a practice going back as far as time itself. A quote from Roman naturalist Pliny the Elder attributes the Persians as the original perfume kings – they used to liberally soak themselves in the stuff to dispel the smell of grime and dirt. For a long time after that, the primary function of perfume was to mask unpleasant smells and show social status. In more recent times, a survey by the Sense of Smell Institute, in collaboration with the *New York Times*, asked men and women the reasons why they wear fragrance; for men it was resoundingly about their attractiveness to others, while for women it seemed to have more to do with pleasing themselves or boosting their self-confidence.

Both effects are backed up with scientific evidence. Firstly, fragrances do make you more confident. Researchers in Japan showed that women were more self-assured in their body language when they were wearing perfume than when they weren't. In the study, thirty-one women were each interviewed by another lady, who was working in cahoots with the scientists. Halfway through the interview they were asked to apply a few spritzes of perfume. The interviews were filmed and observed by a group of eighteen other people, who were watching on a muted TV so could see but not hear what was going on. Once they were wearing the fragrance, the women were seen to be more self-confident; they smiled more and increased their level of eye contact with the interviewer. They also displayed less 'negative' body language, shifting around in their seats less and touching their face and hair less often. The women themselves reported that they felt more relaxed and 'dominant' when they were wearing perfume.

Secondly, when you smell nice you are more attractive. In a similar study, a group of thirty-five male students from Liverpool University were handed a 'new deodorant' in a plain un-branded can, and asked to use it every day. Half the men, however, had been given a can without any aroma or deodorising properties. After a few days, a group of women were asked to judge how attractive the men were, both in photographs and on video. The men were rated as equally attractive when seen static in a picture. But the deodorised group were rated as much fitter on film; displaying self-confident behaviour that resulted in them coming across as more attractive.

Whatever the motivation behind splashing a soupçon of something on yourself in the morning, wearing a fragrance has a huge perceptual and behavioural effect, both on the wearer and on other people. The particular scent you wear depends on personal preference, but different types of aromas have different effects. The classic categorisation of perfumes used by manufacturers and retailers is to divide them into four 'families' – fresh, oriental, floral and woody. Although many nuanced distinctions exist, and many perfumes cross over between categories, it's a useful guide for identifying the character of a scent. Looking at each family, we can see what effects different fragrances have on the wearer and those around them, in order to help select the perfect fragrance for each day.

FRESH

Fragrances that are on the fresh side of the wheel have green outdoor notes and citrusy elements. If you want to be nicer to people, try wearing something with a bit of citrus on your skin. One piece of research asked participants to rate how they felt about people in photographs, while exposing them to low levels of different aromas. When the scent was lemon, the subjects rated the people in the pictures as better looking and more approachable. The researchers found that the effects were greatest when the scent was barely detectable, which suggests that once your morning spritz has dissipated into the background, everyone you meet will appear more congenial and better-looking.

Fresh scents also have a positive energising effect on your mental state, causing a measurable lift in spirits. A study of over 600 women in Germany that mapped personality types to the four fragrance families showed that fresh scents were the common choice of those with more extroverted personalities. Wearing a fresh fragrance will mean you come across as energised and outgoing, and will also increase your appeal to other extroverts. Consider who you might be meeting today and whether their personality will match your scent, in order to help you get along with them.

ORIENTAL

Oriental fragrances have ingredients like vanilla and amber, or woody spices like cinnamon and cardamom. The survey of German women mentioned above, conducted by Joachim Mensing and Christa Beck, showed that Oriental perfumes are the choice of the introvert. Wearing them is seen as an expression of individuality and inner confidence, but not in a way that is aloof or non-inclusive.

Oriental scents exude warmth, and that characteristic gets projected onto the wearer in quite a profound way. Throughout the book we will come across a few instances of this crossover between 'sensorial warmth' – as in warm smells, warm temperature and warm materials – and 'emotional warmth' – being seen as friendly, open and welcoming. As an emotion, warmth has a powerful influence on how much we like or dislike a person or place. Think about how you would react if someone you were about to meet was described as a 'warm' versus a 'cold' person; the difference in your impression of them would be huge. So coming across as warm is beneficial if you want to be seen positively by others, and a warm scent will help massively.

FLORAL

Floral scents reduce stress and can help you think more creatively. Perfumes with floral characteristics promote 'emotional ambivalence' – having mixed emotions about something – which can encourage creative thought. A study by researchers from the University of Washington showed that being in a state of emotional ambivalence promotes the ability to recognise unusual relationships between concepts or find alternative solutions to problems – floral fragrances can help instigate a floaty emotional state where innovative ideas are born.

Floral scents are also physiologically calming. One study that tested a range of fragrances on a group of women showed that they had significantly reduced feelings of stress and anxiety, were more relaxed and felt happier when they were wearing floral perfumes.

WOODY

People who wear woody scents are seen as stable and practical, and they project an air of calm confidence. These aromas also have a physiologically calming effect; a study in Japan found that the scent of cedarwood oil lowered stress and anxiety. With notes like cedar, vetiver and patchouli as their key identifiers, woody fragrances are regarded as the more masculine of the four families, though they are obviously not the exclusive domain of men. I've used woody scents in retail environments ranging from a craft beer shop to car dealerships, in order to signify craft and authenticity; they increase perceptions of 'luxury' and slow people down as they cross the shop floor. These attributes are no different when the scents are on a person; wear woody fragrances when you want to exude a quiet confidence, an air of authenticity and a feeling of emotional warmth.

What fragrance you wear depends on your taste and mood, but it is worth considering how your choice will affect you on a deeper emotional, psychological and physiological level. Wearing fragrances has been shown to have a greater effect on how other people rate your personality   including how sociable, confident and interesting you seem – than other forms of cosmetics, like make-up. It's an historic practice that has profound effects on how you feel and how others feel about you – and can add another sensorial string to your bow.

Breakfast

As you swan into the kitchen, smelling good and dressed to impress, it might be a good idea to do what you can to encourage some good intentions. We should all try to be healthier with what we eat and how we behave, and some of us need all the help we can get. There are things you can do at home in order to sway your behaviour towards the saintly, and the choice of crockery in your cupboards can balance out any lack of indulgence with extra flavour. To begin with, we need a sensory prescription that will encourage healthy decisions.

BRIGHT LIGHT

The first thing to do is turn the lights on bright – and if you're not shrouded in the darkness of winter, open the curtains and get as much daylight in as possible. Bright light encourages us to make healthier food choices: surveys have been conducted in restaurants with lighting ranging from low and sultry to bright daylight, and people always order healthier food in brighter places. A professor called Dipayan Biswas at the University of South Florida has dedicated himself to the study of this effect. Professor Biswas and his team conducted a study in a chain of 'casual restaurants' that is said to have 1,200 outlets in twenty-three countries. On a particular day, two of the outlets in the US had low lighting and two had bright lighting, and in each one they asked customers what they ate and how they felt in terms of their mental alertness. In the brighter restaurants, people felt more alert and chose more vegetables, grilled fish and chicken dishes rather than fried food, beef and pork. The calorific content of people's meals was significantly higher in the low-lit restaurants.

Back in the lab, the team replicated the study – bright or low light conditions, with plain Oreos and the chocolate-covered variety as the food choices. One hundred and thirty-five students were offered the two, and when the light was bright the majority opted for the 'healthy' version.

FRESH, INVIGORATING AROMA

As you'll remember from the Introduction, participants in a study in New Zealand bought more wholefoods when they were exposed to the scent of fresh herbs. In the University of South Florida study mentioned above, they also included a condition that added citrus aroma to the mix. When researchers asked people to choose between a cheesecake and a fruit pot, the results were even greater than just with the lighting – more healthy choices were made with the bright light and citrus smell together. The researchers suggested that we have a propensity to be healthy when we're more mentally alert, and that the combination of bright light and citrus scent had a positively invigorating effect. From a cross-sensory point of view they are completely congruent, which would cause a 'super-additive' effect – making the brightness seem brighter and the citrus zestier.

BE QUIET

You might feel that a bit of vibrant loud music would be congruent with the bright light and the fresh scent. By all means put on some upbeat tunes to coincide with the atmosphere you've created, but keeping the volume low would be preferable. Once again, Dipayan Biswas has been spearheading this area of research. His team measured the lunch choices in a café when different levels and different types of music were playing in the background. Whether the genre was pop, jazz, classical or metal, the results were the same: people ate healthier food when the volume was lower. When they replicated the study in a lab, asking people to choose between fruit salad and chocolate cake, many more people ate the cake when the music was louder. The style of music didn't seem to matter – only the volume did.

Obviously, it's probably a good idea to not tempt yourself. Don't put Professor Biswas's research to the test and lay out a fruit salad and a chocolate cake on the table to see which way you go. If you stock up your cupboards with the good stuff, you won't be in this position. We'll come to how you can resist temptation while walking around the aisles later.

HOW TO ENCOURAGE HEALTHY CHOICES
- **Light** – Bright, and daylight if possible.
- **Aroma** – Fresh and invigorating – fresh herbs and citrus.
- **Sound and music** – Quiet and gentle but upbeat, to keep the alertness levels up.

Now that you've opted to go healthy, there are some things we can do in order to make your breakfast taste more indulgent. What you serve it in can make a big difference – here's a sensory prescription for how to enhance richness, sweetness and indulgence, without the calories.

A SATISFYINGLY WEIGHTY BOWL

For this example of cross-sensory enhancement, I'm going to assume that your breakfast of choice is something like a bowl of yoghurt and granola, but the sensory effect should be the same whatever you're eating. Serving your pile of goodness in a heavier bowl will make it taste richer and more indulgent. When researchers at Oxford University presented students with the same yoghurt in a thin plastic bowl and a heavy porcelain one, the yoghurt in the heavier bowl was rated as better quality, thicker and richer. Even when the same person ate the same yoghurt from the two bowls, one after the other, they thought they were different.

In this example, the feeling of physical weight in your hand and the increased effort it takes to hold the bowl translates to other forms of sensory 'heaviness', in addition to learned emotional associations with what that means. As a result, heavy becomes dense or thick, and also more expensive. This link between weight, taste and quality has been replicated across foods and drink; grab your heaviest bowl out of the cupboard for your breakfast, and pour your coffee into a heavy mug for added richness. As you sit down to dig in, you'll need to hold the bowl in your hands so you can feel its weight. But you shouldn't stop your crockery selection there – if we're going to make this work as best as possible, there are more nuanced choices to be made.

ROUND SHAPES, ROUND TEXTURE

To refer back to our conundrum from the Introduction, if you were presented with a round, fluid shape and an angular, spiky one, which one would be sweeter? Virtually everyone will go for the rounded shape – we relate sweet flavours to curved forms, so eating and drinking out of rounded objects or things with rounded textures increases the perceived sweetness. The shape and texture will also increase how intense or rich a flavour is.

A group of researchers at the University of Twente in the Netherlands recently 3D-printed two identically shaped mugs with different textures, to test the effects on flavour. One was covered in rounded bobbly bits, and the other had a blocky, angular texture. In a supermarket taste test for a fictitious new brand cunningly devised by the team behind the study, the researchers offered shoppers a sample of coffee or hot chocolate from one of the mugs, before asking them to evaluate the taste for qualities including sweetness, bitterness, intensity and pleasantness. Drinks in the round bobbly mug tasted on average around 18 per cent sweeter, while in the angular-textured mug the same drinks tasted up to 27 per cent more bitter and much more intense. If you're trying to cut down on your sugar, avoid drinking from a mug with a rough or angular texture – go for a round bowl and mug, and if possible ones with a smooth rounded texture too.

RED CROCKERY

Here's a good experiment to try at home – make a big pot of coffee, and get out a range of mugs in different colours – if you have them, go for a red, a yellow and a blue one. Pour the coffee into the different mugs, line them up in front of you and taste each one. Do they all taste the same? Reading this without doing the experiment, you may well assume that they will taste identical – after all, they *are* the same. However, by now you should understand that taste isn't just about what's on the palate – other factors are at play. Maybe there's some cross-sensory trickery working on your mind and influencing your taste buds. In quite a few studies that have investigated the influence of colour on taste, it has been shown that food and drink tastes sweeter and richer when it is served from a red receptacle.

I once performed this experiment for BBC Radio 4, with hot chocolate. A programme on politics was exploring how we decide who to vote for, and whether our decision is a result of signals that we pick up without our conscious knowledge – the colour shirt a politician is wearing, perhaps. I was asked to show how we can be influenced by such factors. As the presenter sat in a sound booth, I was in another room, decanting hot chocolate into red, yellow, blue and black mugs. Beforehand, I had recorded a piece saying that I was confident the presenter would choose the red mug. I walked in with the four mugs on a tray and asked her to taste them, commenting on the flavour and quality of each one. First came the yellow one, which she thought was a bit thin. The blue one was slightly better. The red was fuller, nice and sweet. The hot chocolate in the black mug was bitter and not nice. Then I asked which was her favourite, and true to my prediction she chose the red mug, saying the hot chocolate was thicker, richer and better quality.

This advice can make light and healthy food be perceived as sweeter and more indulgent. You can abstain from that extra drizzle of honey on your granola and you no longer need to add that spoonful of sugar to your coffee or tea; a sensorial dietary solution can give you a richer tasting breakfast without the added calories.

HOW TO INCREASE SWEETNESS AND INDULGENCE

- **Colour** – red (a deep, rich red – no wishy-washy pastel hues)
- **Shape** – round
- **Texture** – smooth, bobbly and undulating
- **Weight** – heavy

After you've finished your breakfast, you will hopefully be feeling bright, well fed and ready to go out into the world. Next on the day's agenda is a spot of exercise – but before that, the first of a few brief diversions to look at each sense on its own.

CHAPTER 2

Sight

Throughout this book there will be a short sidestep here and there, taking time out of the daily routine to focus intently on each sense individually. To explore their unique wonders and their role in our multisensory perception of the world. And so it makes sense, excuse the pun, to begin with the one that has been regarded as number one ever since Aristotle said it was. And no one argues with Aristotle. I'm talking about sight.

Our sense of sight will get a bit of a bashing in the sections on scent, sound, taste and touch, but that's because the other senses tend to get overlooked in favour of what we can see. In most aspects of life, our sense of sight and the importance of how things look almost always takes precedence, and is often the only sense that we consider at all. In the design of homes, offices, hospitals, galleries, public spaces, towns and cities, our attention is focused almost entirely on how things look, and hardly ever on what these places should sound like or how they should smell. Films have visual effects budgets of tens of millions, while the budgets for sound and music are a fraction of that – despite the fact that, as David Lynch once said, what you hear is 50 per cent as important as what you see, sometimes more. Restaurants spend millions on the decor before letting the duty manager plug their phone in and play whatever music they fancy. In some ways, this whole book is about how we should pay more attention to the other senses, but that shouldn't detract from the sight's primary role in how we behave and perceive the world around us.

Aristotle's hierarchy of the senses was sight, followed by hearing, smell, taste and touch. A couple of thousand years later, a study at the Faculty of Industrial Design at Delft University in the Netherlands asked a group of consumers which sense they thought was the most important as they evaluated forty-five different types of products, ranging from kettles to washing detergent. The ranking of the senses came out as sight, touch, smell, hearing and taste. Slightly different to Aristotle; but both agree on number one.

We are physically designed to be sight-dominant. Our eyes are positioned at the front of our brains. What we 'see' is light; our 'vision' is what our brain tells us we are seeing. It's the process of how we derive meaning from what our eyes pick up. So, in that way it is a very different, learned sense. Rather than something physical like the molecules in the air that make up a smell, or the vibrations and changes in pressure that we translate into sound, vision is the culmination of a complex set of neurological functions that involve a multitude of skills. We are able to hear almost as wide a range of sounds when we are born as we can as an adult, and we are able to pick up as many aromas. But as babies we can only see around eight inches in front of our faces, and our perception of colour is pretty much black and white. The cones in our retina, which pick up the millions of colours that we can perceive, don't start developing for at least a couple of months after we are born, but as our sight develops, our vision begins to take over and our eyes become incredibly sophisticated sensory receptors. Many researchers agree that about 80 per cent of our cognitive processing of our environment is through sight.

Even when another sense is seemingly dominant, like taste when we're eating, our sight has a huge influence on what is being perceived. For instance, in a research study entitled 'A Taste of Kandinsky', conducted at Oxford University's Crossmodal Research Laboratory, sixty participants were each served a plate of food. The dish was the same for everyone, but it was presented in one of three ways – regular, neat and 'art-inspired'. The 'regular' dish had all the ingredients bunched in the middle of the plate, in one of those cheffy rings. The 'neat' presentation saw the constituent elements of the dish laid out in neat lines (not particularly appetising, but at least you could see what you were getting). And for the 'art-inspired' version, the dish was arranged to look like *Painting Number 201* by the eponymous Kandinsky. Of the sixty participants, twenty were served with the food presented in each way, with none of them aware that other people were being served the dish in any other way.

The diners were asked to complete a questionnaire about the food before they ate it and then again afterwards, judging how much they liked the presentation, how good they expected it to taste, and how much they enjoyed eating it. The results for each dish were drastically different: the artistic dish was liked a lot more, the food was rated as tastier and people were willing to pay more for it. The 'regular' presentation was second most popular, and the 'neat' arrangement came third. The differences between what people expected the food to taste like and how they rated it afterwards were interesting. People eating the Kandinsky dish expected it to be really tasty, and said it was even tastier once they had eaten it, whereas ratings of the 'regular' version went down. And the one with the ingredients laid out neatly tasted exactly as people predicted.

Something about the visual beauty of Kandinsky's composition improved the taste of the food, which might mean that we all have an inherent appreciation of art. As the researchers ventured, 'the art-inspired presentation of the food could have been an edible rendition of the message originally intended by Kandinsky on the canvas'.

Either way, this study not only showed that sight can affect taste and that the aesthetic value of something can tantalise our taste buds as much as our eyes, but also, as the 'neat' condition proved, that if we see an ingredient we recognise, we know what it will taste like. Our sense of sight primes us for expectation, based on our past experience. And what you see is what you get, even if it isn't; if you see something and expect it to be one thing but it turns out to be another, sight's dominance will prevail and you will get what your eyes told you.

Another good example of this was when a group of wine experts got duped into thinking white wine was red wine, when it was simply white wine dyed red. In 2001, while working on his PhD at the University of Bordeaux, Frédéric Brochet presented fifty-four wine students with two glasses of the same white wine, one of which was dyed with flavourless red food colouring. The students described the white-white wine using the sort of terms you would expect – 'floral', 'honey', 'peach' and 'lemon'. But then, they overwhelmingly described the identical red-white wine using words usually reserved for red – 'raspberry', 'cherry', 'cedar' and 'chicory'. As Brochet put it in an article in *The Times*, 'They were expecting to taste a red wine and so they did ... About 2 or 3 per cent of people can detect the white wine flavour, but invariably they have little experience of wine culture. Connoisseurs tend to fail to do so. The more training they have, the more mistakes they make because they are influenced by the colour of the wine.'

Colours prime us to expect a range of qualities about everything around us, based on the meanings we attribute to each one. A lot of these assumptions are largely universal and can drift into the abstract. To use a popular example: which colour do you think is heaviest, red or yellow? Most people will say red is heavier than yellow – like lemons being fast, this is one of the most often cited cross-modal correspondences that reveal our multisensory world of perception. But people who have been blind almost since birth and have never seen a colour at all will also say that red is heavier than yellow.

Researchers in Italy and Belgium took forty-six seeing individuals and forty-six early-blind individuals and asked them a series of cross-modal conundrums, such as 'Is a lemon fast or slow?', 'Which colour is heavier, red or yellow?' and 'Is a boulder sweet or sour?' (The answer to this last one is supposedly that boulders are sour.) Because colour can only be experienced through sight, the red-yellow question is the one that separates the two groups. Around 90 per cent of the sighted participants answered that red was heavy, and 70 per cent of the visually impaired group did too. This result flags the important question about sensory perception that I mentioned in the Introduction, regarding whether such associations are learned through language and experience or hard-wired versions of the synaesthesia that we all have within us. The study backs up both arguments, depending on how you look at it. Early-blind people have never seen red, but have heard the word used metaphorically and have heard the colour described. But also, even if they have never experienced the colour visually, there still may be an inbuilt synaesthetic link within them that red is heavy, and our language and the emotional connotations of red may have developed to reflect that association.

Our sight is the sense that is in charge in many situations, while always being totally connected to the others – from colours priming us for certain sensory expectations to the McGurk effect, where sight is shown to have complete 'sensory dominance' over sound. It is worth watching a video of it, as it has to be seen to be believed. The discovery happened by accident in 1976, while the researchers Harry McGurk and John MacDonald were conducting a study about language development in infants. They were overdubbing a film of someone talking to camera while playing a different soundtrack, when they noticed something amazing. On screen you might see someone repeatedly mouthing 'fa, fa, fa' to camera, but the soundtrack playing is of someone repeating the sound 'ba, ba, ba'. With two incongruent pieces of sensory information, the brain has to decide which to go with – and sight wins. Your brain makes you hear 'fa, fa, fa' because that's what you're seeing, even though you are actually hearing 'ba, ba, ba'. Close your eyes and you hear 'ba', but look at the screen and you hear 'fa'. It's crazy and you cannot stop it, even though you know it's happening.

While we're looking at people's faces, it is worth dwelling for a moment on how we are visually geared to pick up information from other people. Our brain even has an area in the visual cortex designed to process faces. As a baby, a human face is more attention-grabbing than anything, and as soon as we are able to move around, we are evolutionarily predisposed to crawl towards a happy smiling face rather than a shifty-looking one. We are thought to judge people's personality just by looking at their face, in as little as one-tenth of a second.

Two Princeton University psychologists, Janine Willis and Alexander Todorov, showed how these snap judgements almost always reflect the evaluations made after a longer period of time. They showed people images of various faces for periods of between one-tenth of a second and one second, asking them to respond as quickly as possible to certain questions, such as: Is this person competent? Or likeable? How attractive are they? A separate control group was shown the same images with no timeframe, and most of the snap judgements made after one-tenth of a second were the same as the consensus view of the control group.

The trait that people were most confident in attributing to the faces was 'trust'; round features, big eyes and baby-like characteristics make people look more trustworthy. In a review of 506 small claims court hearings, a group of researchers identified that people were more likely to win, whether they were plaintiff or defendant, if they were baby-faced or attractive – because of our innate visual prejudices, there is no such thing as a fair trial, as long as the jurors get to see the people involved. Equally, a square face and chiselled jaw will mean that we think the person is more dominant and competent.

In 2005, a study managed to predict the outcomes of American senatorial elections with 70 per cent accuracy, by showing members of the public photographs of the candidates and asking them to judge how competent they thought they were. Those who were judged as competent by their face alone were more likely to go on to win, a pattern that was later corroborated in other cultures.

We seem to have developed a visual language of facial recognition that influences our emotional judgement of people, before we are even consciously aware of what those things really mean. And because it's evolutionarily wired in us to do this, there's no escaping it. Humans are such a social species that it makes sense for us to be able to quickly assess if someone is friend or foe. The problem, though, is that our snap judgements and prejudices are often wrong. People with chiselled jaws aren't all competent, and round-faced individuals are certainly not all trustworthy. Professor Alexander Todorov from Princeton University explains that, perhaps because we're now exposed to so many faces, our visual cortices have gone for the simplest groupings and attributed certain features to certain personality traits, but as a result we're susceptible to the worst type of visual stereotyping. The only thing we can do about it is hang out with as many different-looking people as possible, of all races, creeds, colours, face shapes and features – and train ourselves to adjust our visual prejudices by using our newly acquired learned experience to question our innate snap judgement.

Our sense of sight is usually how we first encounter anyone or anything. It is 'the primer' that sets up what we think we're going to get through the other senses, and from that point on it has an impact on them. But the other senses are always there too, sending information this way and that to the others. Aristotle got it wrong when he said our senses are all separate; all our experiences are multisensory, and we are starting from an incorrect position if we try to explain something with the assumption that our senses operate individually. As this book will hopefully prove, if all the information coming in from every sense is congruent – fitting and working together – then the effect is greater and enjoyment is enhanced. From food and drink, to your office or living room, choosing the right colours, shapes, lighting and visuals for the right situations can have a hugely beneficial effect. Throughout the following chapters I'll cover as many examples of this as possible, but let's get on with our day – it's time for some exercise.

CHAPTER 3

Exercise

The best time to get your daily dose of exercise is either between 7am and 8am or between 1pm and 4pm. Scheduling your workout for these times will help shift your body clock to a more natural timeframe, in a similar way that sleeping out under the stars aligned the circadian rhythms of the Colorado campers we met in Chapter 1. This 'phase-shifting' effect and the idea that there are times of the day when exercise has the biggest impact are pretty recent discoveries. In 2019, scientists from Arizona State University and the University of California recruited around a hundred people of varying ages for a study in which they were made to run on a treadmill for an hour at specific points throughout the morning – 1, 4, 7 or 10am, and the same in the afternoon or evening – at 1, 4, 7 or 10pm. The research team measured the participants' melatonin levels before and after the workouts. The people who exercised at 7am, 1pm and 4pm managed to move their melatonin onset – the wave of sleep-inducing hormone that can hit us after we wake up – to where it should naturally be, a couple of hours earlier when they were still asleep, helping to combat feelings of sleep inertia.

Exercising later on in the evening, between 7pm and 10pm, had the opposite effect, delaying the melatonin onset even further. This is a negative effect for those on a standard daily routine, but could be handy for late-night shift workers. By exercising in the evening before you start work, you can help align your circadian rhythm to your otherwise unnatural hours.

If you can't make the morning 7–8am window, the afternoon slot may be easier, with the 1–4pm window being handy at weekends to combat what is called 'social jetlag' – the consequence of being in a normal routine all week and then staying out till two in the morning on a Friday night. You sleep in until eleven on Saturday morning and then struggle to get up early on the following Monday. If you want to keep that weekend lie-in and manage to get back on track by the start of the working week, force yourself to do some exercise at 1pm or 4pm on Saturday and Sunday – you should have yourself realigned by Monday morning and wake up feeling dandy.

For the purposes of our day, however, today's exercise will be the morning shift. From a sensory point of view, exercise is about making sure everything in your environment is aligned with your state of mind, emotions and the activity that you're getting involved in. Working out is about making yourself feel active, motivated and confident, and surrounding yourself with sensorially congruent elements that help support this feeling will help bring those behaviours to the fore.

Getting Ready

Let's assume that you arrive at the gym, head to the changing room and are about to get yourself ready for a workout. It could be a lone run, a group class or maybe you're here for a competitive sport. Obviously, you don't have much control over the environment in the changing rooms or the gym itself, but you are in control of your clothing and paraphernalia.

WEAR BRIGHT COLOURS AND GEOMETRIC, ANGULAR PATTERNS

When it comes to style, 'active-wear' has a lot to answer for; always so garish and covered with crazy patterns and colours. Well, there is a justification for such sartorial crimes; if we relate the notions of being active to something visual, we come to angularity and brightness – sharp shapes and loud colours. Angular shapes are dynamic and are used to represent action, precision, and convey aggression – a series of studies have showed that a downward 'V' shape reflects a person's face when they're angry, and pops out of visual designs because we're evolutionarily wired to detect threat. Returning to the idea of enclothed cognition, if we want to feel energised and sharp we should wear bright colours and outfits with sharp, angular patterns.

WEAR RED IF YOU'RE COMPETING

If you wear red, you are statistically more likely to perform better at a sport. A group of researchers looked at the outcomes of boxing, taekwondo, Greco-Roman wrestling and freestyle wrestling matches in the 2004 Olympics. Before each bout began, the athletes were randomly assigned red or blue as their fighting colour, with the flip of a coin. The results showed that they were about 75 per cent more likely to win if they were allocated the red corner – sixteen out of the twenty-one rounds were won by the person wearing red. The effect was greatest when the competitors were evenly matched; in those instances, it seemed to be the determinate factor.

It's not just in hand-to-hand combat that this colour-related psychological effect has an impact. The same group of researchers also looked at football teams in the 2004 UEFA Champions League. They compared five teams who wore a predominantly red shirt for some games and played other matches in an alternative strip that was either white or blue. All five teams scored more goals and won more games when they were wearing their red kit.

The researchers believe that, in the eyes of your competition, by playing in red you will be viewed as more dangerous and forceful; by contrast, those playing in white or blue may feel more timid than they would otherwise be, thus swinging the balance of power in your favour.

CLOTHES THAT MAKE THE RIGHT SOUNDS

Everything you hear affects your emotions and your behaviour. However, the sounds of objects, products and clothes are largely ignored, or at least are not utilised to bring added benefit to what we're doing. An example from my work was an electric toothbrush I worked on recently. The manufacturers hadn't considered that the sound could make a difference, but we showed that if the motor was slightly louder but with a softer more muted sound, people felt the brush was simultaneously more powerful and gentler on their gums. Consequently, the brush's sound was given (almost) as much attention as its visual appearance.

You don't usually want your clothes to make much noise at all, but there are materials that you could wear during exercise to bring a sound-induced emotional boost to your performance. Think about the difference between wearing a top that fastens with poppers and one that uses Velcro, and the sound of pulling it open as you push yourself forwards. The pitiful pop pop of poppers or the forceful and invigorating tearing crunch of Velcro? The loud abrasive noise will give you a burst of energy, helping you to accelerate towards victory.

If you are dressed in a soft material that produces muted

sounds as you move your body, you would feel less dynamic than if you could hear the high-pitched sheen of a synthetic fabric. The former sort of material might be beneficial for something that involves keeping a steady rhythm – a long-distance run, cycle or row, perhaps – but the crinkling of a synthetic fabric is more suited to sharper movements and bursts of energy. It's something to consider when choosing your outfit. Think about what state of mind you want to be in to boost your performance, and then about the sounds that will encourage it.

WATER BOTTLE

A water bottle is an object that will be by your side throughout your workout, and we can apply the sensory approach to its design so it is congruent with what you're doing and with everything else around you. If this is a bottle that you will be picking up and putting down in between bursts of energy, it should ideally be relatively heavy, in order to transfer its physical weight into feelings of power and confidence. Like the heavy bowls at breakfast or the feel of a heavy piece of jewellery, weight conveys notions of quality, strength and solidity.

The bottle should be metallic, so that it feels cold and fresh to the touch. These sensations will give you a feeling of activity, the opposite of a hot water bottle covered in a woolly cosy. There should also be an angularity to the shape, so that it feels more dynamic; this will enhance the fresh flavour of the liquid inside.

MINTY WATER

A couple of drops of peppermint in your water has been shown to increase performance during exercise, by reducing blood pressure and increasing respiratory rate and capacity. Sports scientists in Iran put a group of male students on a daily routine of drinking 0.05ml of peppermint essential oil diluted in 500ml of water. When they measured the men's fitness levels and performance on a treadmill after just ten days, their performance and lung function had improved, it took longer for them to get tired and their resting and post-exercise heart rates were lower.

A SPRITZ OF LEMONGRASS, OR OTHER SCENTS WITH MOVEMENT

For a pre-exercise motivational spritz of aroma, there are ingredients that actually feel like they are moving. Perfumers use them as stimulating 'top notes' that give a sense of energy to their fragrances. Lemongrass is one such ingredient, along with 'aldehydes', types of synthetic aroma that are added to fragrances to give them a fizz when you first smell them; the classic Chanel No. 5 was one of the first scents to use them. These types of scents have effervescence and energy, and lemongrass is particularly great because it fits perfectly with the sensory world we have created so far, being a fresh, zesty and lively aroma. A small spray in the air as you finish getting ready will give you a psychological boost as you burst out of the changing room doors.

THE POWER OF YOUR SENSES

A SENSORY PRESCRIPTION FOR PRE-WORKOUT PREP

- **Colour** – Wear red if you're competing or want to make yourself feel more confident and powerful. Bright colours are good for energy.
- **Patterns** – Go for clothes with crazy angular patterns for some enclothed cognition that will increase your active, energetic vibe.
- **Sound** – Think about the sound your clothes make and how they can help with what you're doing.
- **Shapes** – Again, angular and solid, sharp forms for anything you have with you, including your water bottle.
- **Taste** – Put a bit of peppermint oil, or maybe even some fresh mint leaves, in your water for a physiological benefit.
- **Scent** – Use an effervescent aroma such as lemongrass to give you an energetic lift.

Working Out

The most important sensory accompaniment for exercise is music, and all gyms like to pump out playlists of high-octane tunes to keep up the energy levels. Music is proven to be incredibly effective in helping you get more out of your time, whether you are in the gym or out and about. There are a few proven points as to what will work best for you.

LISTEN TO YOUR MUSIC, NOT THE GYM'S

Unless you have a penchant for the type of dance-pop that makes up most gyms' musical repertoire, playing music that you yourself like produces more positive results than listening to someone else's choices.

In a straightforward 1.5-mile running test, students from Texas A&M University ran faster when they were listening to their own music, achieving a better result from the same amount of effort. Another study at the Human Performance Laboratory at California State University showed similar results: scientists measured the take-off velocity of a group of men doing squat jumps while they listened to playlists of their own design through speakers in the room. When the subjects put their music of choice on and began squat jumping their hearts out, they accelerated faster, had more power in their lift-off, and reported increased feelings of vigour! They did not, however, jump any higher.

The reason that listening to your own music is better can be partly explained by the fact that you are more likely to get lost in it, rather than focusing on the passing of every second and the repetition of exercise. Your own music also tends to make you happy, and listening to music that you like helps you relax, which relaxes your muscles and allows greater blood flow. It can consequently have what's called a 'psychobiological' impact and improve your exercise capabilities.

FAST AND LOUD OR SLOW AND LOW

A study conducted in the UK sought to discover what the ideal tempo and volume of an accompanying workout playlist would be, in terms of increasing performance. Participants ran for ten minutes at a time, first with no music, then with slow and quiet music, followed by slow and loud, fast and quiet, and fast and loud tunes. Performance was better when there was music playing, and people ran fastest when it was fast and loud.

But there was another discovery that was quite interesting. The participants pushed themselves further, increasing the treadmill speed as they ran, when the music was fast and loud or slow and quiet, but not when it was fast and quiet or slow and loud. This shows that if you do prefer slower-paced music, if you listen to it quietly you will get a better workout. Conversely, if your preference is for faster music, make it loud. The most plausible reason for this is that the two combinations go well together – we equate high energy with high volume. When the tempo and volume match, our mind is not alerted by the strange incongruity and has no need to use energy dealing with what's wrong. Instead we are able to accept the sensorial stimulus, letting it breeze over us and do all the good things I mentioned above – distract attention and make you happy.

So, if you want to go faster, play loud and fast music. If you're happy with a little less speed and a lower heart rate, play some slower tunes and set the volume low.

ROUGH BASS AND CRISP, CLEAN TREBLE

Finally on music, there are some qualities that will help further enhance your performance. This is what in my industry we call a 'sonic brief': guidelines for the sort of music a brand should use in order to communicate their values and personality. If we think of 'exercise' as the brand and follow our sensory prescription, the personality we want to communicate is confident and powerful and the benefits are that it makes you feel active, fresh and energetic. Therefore, the 'sonic brief' would be:

- A good amount of bass, to drive power and confidence.
- Low-end sounds should have texture, to enhance confidence and attitude.
- Top-end frequencies should be clean, crisp and clear, to bring freshness.
- Keep the sound tight, without tons of reverb or space in the mix.
- Notes should be played strongly and staccato for an active, sharper feel.

As for the smelly side of workouts, gyms tend to already have their signature aroma, and there is something to be said for not trying to change it beyond all recognition. For many of us, the heady concoction of sweaty Lycra and disinfectant wipes will already be ingrained in our psyche as a sensorial memory and will fire up your workout juices as soon as a waft hits you. Although it's not particularly pleasant, it's almost as evocative as fresh coffee or baked bread.

However, for personal benefit, having a scent in your vicinity has been shown to have a similar effect to music in diverting attention from 'the burn', meaning you can push yourself a little further. One piece of research asked people to squeeze a hand grip while they had a scent strip under their nose; a control group attempted the challenge with no scent. The results showed that people with the scent were able to maintain their grip for longer – they said they focused less on time passing or on the pain of sustaining the squeeze.

PEPPERMINT AROMA

Lavender and peppermint were the aromas used in the study mentioned above; while both were effective, peppermint is the ultimate choice for a workout. Spray a little on your towel or on yourself as you work out. As we saw earlier, when imbibed it increases lung capacity and consequently assists your exercise performance. The cooling sensation when you smell it helps you breathe and cools you down.

Peppermint also improves precision. A study in the Philippines showed that people playing darts were much more accurate when they had inhaled some peppermint scent. Not that darts actually constitutes any form of exercise (and if you class it as a workout, you're in trouble). The study took one hundred non-dart-playing students and got them to sit for two minutes while smelling cotton wool imbued with either lavender or peppermint essential oil (a control group just sat there for two minutes, doing nothing). Then they played darts, and the students that had smelled the peppermint aroma were more accurate and consistent and reported feeling less anxious. It's a whimsical study, but the results suggest that having a sniff or a sip of something peppermint-flavoured before you shoot some hoops or serve in a tennis match might give you an extra edge.

When you use a scent in this way, the trick is to stick with it and use it every time you exercise. By building up an association, it will bring back the right feelings as soon as you catch a waft; then you can use it to bring you into the right mental state whenever you need to. If you are ever finding it difficult to muster the will power to get yourself out and about, a surreptitious sniff of your chosen scent might do the trick.

WORK OUT WITH OTHER, FITTER PEOPLE

More often than not, exercise is performed in groups – whether that's at spin, body sculpt or cross-fit classes or in any other number of activities. The benefits are clear: you push yourself further when people are looking and are less likely to bail out earlier when you're not on your own. We naturally strive for social acceptance, which means that we always do our best to keep up with the pack – a phenomenon sometimes referred to as 'social comparison theory'. A study at Michigan State University proved its impact on exercise motivation. They asked participants to do a plank on their own and then alongside a 'virtual partner' on a screen, which was programmed to be better than the participants. On average, the participants held their planks for 24 per cent longer when they were up against the superior digital competitor.

Sometimes this effect can be negative rather than beneficial; we strive to adapt to the abilities of the people around us, whether they're better or worse than us, in order to fit in. When a study assigned exercise partners to participants, instructing them to either claim extreme fitness or to behave like they were seriously unfit, the unwitting subjects either upped their game or put in less effort accordingly. The trick, therefore, is to either find yourself an exercise partner who is fitter than you, or a class of highly motivated individuals to get involved with.

HIGH FIVE YOUR FELLOW EXERCISERS

In sport, touching is good when it comes to group and personal performance. If you play in a team or exercise in a group, you should high five or fist bump as much as possible. Researchers at the University of California in Berkeley analysed the 2008–9 season of the American NBA, looking at how much teams touched during each game. They found that those players who were more touchy-feely early on in the season were always much better off, both individually and as a team, further down the line. Over the whole season, increased amounts of interpersonal touching improved performance categorically. The researchers believe it increases feelings of social togetherness and collaboration, which is imperative in team sport. It also gives individuals a feeling of self-worth, in addition to increased notions of warmth and trust from their teammates.

LOOK AT GREEN NATURE, WHETHER REAL OR AN IMAGE

Sports scientists use the term 'green exercise' to describe the act of performing physical activity in a natural environment, and the physical and psychological benefits of it are becoming increasingly recognised. But a study conducted at the School of Biological Sciences in the University of Essex showed that simply looking at nature (and not even the real thing) can be almost as good as being out and about.

The researchers took a point-of-view film of someone cycling through a woodland and made three versions: one that was black and white, one that was given a red tint and a third that was left unchanged, full of lush, green trees. They then projected the films onto a screen that was placed in front of an exercise bike, so that it would feel as though participants were cycling along the treelined road. A group pedalled for five minutes at a steady pace to each of the three films, during which their heart rate was monitored. Their moods were captured by answering a 'Profile of Mood States' questionnaire, where you respond to how you feel on a scale between 'not at all' and 'very' to words like 'lively', 'active', 'angry' or 'confused'.

When cycling with the 'natural' version of the film, the participants' performance and mood was much better. They also had lower levels of perceived exertion; they felt less tired and could go for longer. By contrast, both the black and white and the red films had a negative effect on participants' moods, with the red version making them angry. For the best benefits of 'green exercise', you should ideally run or cycle among nature. Otherwise, try to work out in the gym in front of a window, looking out onto a tree or two; you might also try exercising in front of a tablet showing a POV film of nature. If you're into cycling and like buying all the gear, then whatever you do don't buy any wraparound sunglasses that have a red tint, or any tint for that matter. You'll be doing your cycle a disservice and will finish stressed out.

DAYLIGHT

Being outside isn't just about the greenery – it's also the light. It has been shown that aerobic capacity improves when you are physically active outdoors and in natural light. Plus, referring back our circadian rhythms, exercising in natural daylight gets you more in sync than being outside and doing nothing (although that is still preferable to being indoors all the time).

Three sports scientists in Korea conducted a study to prove this definitively, when they asked a group of participants to follow a different daily routine for five days at a time, with a week's break in between to 'reset the clock'. The routines were:

1. Be outdoors for thirty minutes each day, but no exercise.
2. Indoor aerobic exercise for thirty minutes each day.
3. Outdoor aerobic exercise for thirty minutes each day.
4. No exercise and stay indoors.

As you would have predicted, in the fourth condition, the subjects' sleep was quite disturbed; they went to bed later, woke up later and felt groggier. In both of the routines that involved being outdoors – 1 and 3 – the subjects' sleep improved. But routine 3, which allowed the subjects to exercise outdoors, yielded the best results. The subjects fell asleep the quickest, their melatonin levels were higher during sleep (rather than after they woke up) and they slept a pretty perfect seven and a half hours, feeling well-rested each morning.

Sadly, it's not always possible to get outside, or even have a window looking out over a park – we mainly have to make do with what is available at our local gym. But when you are able to, just heading to the local park for exercise will be beneficial – the combination of natural light, green nature and exercise is the Holy Trinity.

BRIGHT LIGHT

There is one visual element that most gyms get right: brightness. Gyms are almost always filled with high-level strip lighting, and bright light can be the best alternative to being outdoors. When researchers measured people's exercise performance in different lighting conditions, they found there was a sweet spot of around 5000K, when the lights are pretty bright and pure white, but not blaringly so. The study, which was conducted in Japan, involved asking a handful of fit individuals to exercise on an exercise bike for fifteen minutes and then rest for twenty minutes, in one of three lighting settings and while being measured by an EEG monitor and reporting on their feelings. At a relatively dim 3000K – about the equivalent of a sixty-watt bulb – the subjects' focus and attention was not the best. In really bright 7000K blue-white light, they felt less relaxed, more tired and took longer to recover. In the pure white light, participants' feelings of motivation were highest.

A SENSORY PRESCRIPTION FOR A BETTER WORKOUT

- **Music** – Choose your own music if you can – it diverts your attention and makes you happy. Fast music will help you go faster, but put it on loud; if you prefer slow music, listen to it at a quieter volume. Choose music with heavy bass and sharp, crisp sounds.

- **Scent** – Spray some peppermint on your towel or on yourself before you begin exercising.
- **Visual** – look at nature, whether it's real or not. You might even place an iPad playing a point-of-view film of travelling through nature in front of your treadmill.
- **Light** – Daylight is the best choice, but otherwise exercise in white light – 5000K – for the best physical and mental effects.
- **People** – Try to work out with people who are fitter than you. Find a motivational partner to work out with, or take a group class with people who look like they know what they're doing.
- **Touch** – A high five or a fist bump makes everyone feel better about themselves.
- **Other** – Work out outdoors if you can – the combination of nature, exercise and natural daylight is hugely beneficial.

Recovery

As soon as you step off the treadmill or stop whatever exercise you've been doing, it is important to cool down. We're all aware of the need for some stretches and a drink of water, but a sensory cool down is essential too. After a workout, your levels of cortisol – the stress hormone – are higher than usual, which helps as an anti-inflammatory and aids muscle recovery. So keep up the fast tunes for about three minutes. After that, you want to start decreasing your cortisol levels, otherwise your body will be left in fight-or-flight mode for too long, which can tire you out and cause unnecessary stress. It's time for a change in pace.

SLOW MUSIC

After you have cooled down, you need to switch to music with a much slower tempo. A study at Brunel University showed that when participants listened to super-slow music – of around 70bpm – for twenty to thirty minutes after exercising, their cortisol levels returned to normal more quickly and they felt more relaxed; when they kept listening to fast music, their cortisol levels and feelings of stress went up. The professor behind the study, Costas Karageorghis, suggests listening to a transitional music playlist that gradually slows your fast-paced exercise music to the beneficial slow tempo, and then continues with the mellow mood while you get dressed and carry on with your day.

As a guide to the type of music you should listen to, longer songs are better because there is less jarring transition between tracks. The use of soothing instruments helps – soft woodwinds and horns are top of Professor Karageorghis's list. And the use of natural sounds such as birdsong can also help, taking us back to the connection we had with the sounds of nature at the start of our day.

LOW LIGHT

Along with the mellow music, you ideally want the light as you get changed after exercising to follow suit. The light study mentioned above showed that people recovered better from bouts of exercise in the warmer low light of around 3000K (similar to a normal home lightbulb). In a dream scenario, there could be separate changing rooms for before and after exercise – a bright one to motivate you when you're getting ready and a warmer, dimmer one to help you recover more quickly afterwards.

EUCALYPTUS

Keeping up the cool and mint-scented theme, the peppermint that is in your water bottle and on your towel will prove a good post-workout scent, helping your breathing and lowering your blood pressure. Eucalyptus is a scent that has anti-inflammatory, pain-relieving benefits – in a review of the use of aromatherapy in pain relief conducted by neuroscientists at the California University of Science and Medicine, eucalyptus was shown to significantly reduce pain perception and blood pressure and ease muscle tension. Take a bottle of eucalyptus oil into the shower with you and add a couple of drops to your soap, or purchase a body wash that contains the real thing.

THE POWER OF YOUR SENSES

A SENSORY PRESCRIPTION FOR YOUR POST-WORKOUT RECOVERY

- **Music** – Switch to slow music (of around 70bpm) to dispel cortisol, but not until you've taken time to cool down after your workout.
- **Light** – Recover from exercise in lower, warm lighting of around 3000K, or the equivalent of a sixty-watt bulb.
- **Scent** – Using eucalyptus oil while you shower can open up your airway and calm your muscles.

You should now leave the gym feeling motivated, fresh and on your way to recovery, while still listening to your slow music playlist. It's time to head off for a multisensorial day at work. But only after another quick single-sense interlude.

CHAPTER 4

Sound

I don't think our sense of hearing is given enough credit these days. I say these days, as if back in the 1800s it was lauded as a miracle of humanity and ear statues were erected all over the country, which isn't the case. What I mean is, we are a very visually focused society, and the impact that sound has on our lives often seems underrated.

Maybe that's because we spend our lives surrounded by sound. The modern world produces a constant drone of motors, engines, hums, rings, alerts and noises that our ears have become accustomed to, so it's no wonder that we shut ourselves off from our sonic environment. If we were to open our ears to everything that's going on around us, we'd go crazy. Auditory academics and philosophers including R. Murray Schafer and Jean-François Augoyard have coined a term for the noise that surrounds us – 'the soundscape' – and refer to it as a living, breathing organism that should be preserved as a record of its time.

Back in the 1800s, the soundscape dramatically changed with the onset of the Industrial Revolution. Before then, our countryside and cities were filled with the clopping of horses' hooves and peasant women selling bread. When steam engines let out their monstrous roars the world changed forever, raising the volume by about 100 decibels. People began shouting for the very first time and saying 'Sorry, I didn't hear you'. And so here we are, with aeroplanes forever flying overhead, cars in perpetual motion and the ubiquitous whirring and beeping of fridges, washing machines and dishwashers that fill the sonic backdrop of our lives.

Although we don't focus on them, the sounds around us exert a huge influence over our state of mind and our behaviour. Background noise can be comforting, distracting or performance-enhancing, but if the soundscape is too loud it dulls your other senses. For instance, when background noise is over a certain volume our ability to pick up the taste of saltiness and umami drastically drops off. The classic situation is on an aeroplane, where in-flight food is made saltier to compensate for the noise; if you ate those meals at home, they would taste really salty.

We are also less productive, creative and socially responsible in loud environments. In 2018, the World Health Organization acknowledged that noise pollution is one of the top environmental risks to health and well-being. This is because loud noise initiates the release of stress hormones, which cause a fight-or-flight mechanism that affects our self-control. A study at Aarhus University in Denmark by Timo Hener states that a one-decibel rise in noise levels in public spaces equates to a 2.6 per cent rise in physical assaults, mostly between strangers. Hener estimates that a one-decibel reduction in noise levels would avoid 18,000 assaults in the US and Europe every year.

Too little noise, however, can feel uncomfortable. We are always in the presence of some kind of sound; in the home a constant low-level hum emanates from every appliance. We only become aware of these sounds when they stop, and there's nothing as noticeable as the disappearance of a sound that you didn't know was there. When the fridge or boiler suddenly stops doing whatever it was doing for a moment, silence appears as loudly as a klaxon going off.

People say 'silence is golden', but true silence can be bloody terrifying. An 'anechoic chamber' is a room that's suspended on springs, its walls covered with an extreme version of the soundproof foam that's used in recording studios. They are the most silent places on earth – all outside noise is nullified and the sound inside is dull and dead. If you spend a few seconds inside one of these places, you lose your sense of space and your balance starts to go a bit funny. A short while longer and you start to hear the inner workings of your body – the pulse in your neck and the blood pumping around your ears become deafening.

This extreme example reminds us that we're used to always having sound around us. Background noise is used artificially in many environments to aid concentration or relaxation. White noise machines that produce a blast of all the frequencies across the sonic spectrum, like a tuned-out radio, are often used to reduce distraction and enhance productivity in offices, and spas play the calming sounds of whale song to put their customers in a state of relaxation.

Using functional or generic sounds is one thing, but using sounds that have a greater emotional connection to us has much more potential; after all, we are 'feeling machines' and engaging our emotions and memories will help us more. Think about the sort of sounds that surround you when you feel relaxed and comfortable, or the soundscapes of your past that have emotional resonance – they can be used far more effectively to help change your state of mind or repel distraction. I've always had a strong emotional affinity to the ting-ting noise of boats' rigging knocking against their masts in the wind; it reminds me of the marina on the south coast of England where my dad had a boat, and of happy times fishing for crabs from the jetty. To this day I find the sound instantly settling, but birdsong or traffic noise might be your personal whale song. The drone of fridges and heating pipes can be an effective way to avoid silence in a more emotionally 'warm' way than cold white noise, as they are sounds that symbolise the atmosphere of a home rather than an office.

I'm reminded of John Cusack's character in *Midnight in*

the Garden of Good and Evil taking a recording of New York traffic with him when he visits Savannah, to play as he goes to sleep – it's his own personal lullaby of familiar noise, without which he can't drift off. An example of this for me is a soundscape I made for my little boy Linus, before he was born. I read up about the sensory world that he was immersed in while in the womb. Hearing is one of the first senses a foetus develops, along with smell and taste, and they live in a sonic world for the last four and a half months of pregnancy, of their mother's voice and the gurgling of their watery surroundings. In an attempt to help him sleep well, I attempted to craft a sleep-enhancing soundtrack from the sounds I thought might be most familiar and relaxing to him. I recorded his mother's voice calmly mumbling, and the deep guttural snore of our bulldog, Dudley, who would always sit in her lap when she lay on the sofa. I made the noises sound muffled and added an artist's impression of the sound of being inside his mum, attempting to recreate what he might hear. After Linus was born, I would play the soundscape next to his cot whenever he wasn't going to sleep easily, and he would stop crying straight away. I know babies tend to respond to constant noise, and white noise machines can be used as sleep aids. A friend who had a baby girl at the same time would put a radio tuned into static next to her cot; that didn't work for Linus, but the soundscape I made did. I firmly believe that the sounds he was hearing were familiar and had already been associated in his mind with feelings of calm, safety and warmth, a personalised soundscape created out of the sounds in his environment when he had felt most at ease.

Background sound isn't just about affecting our well-being and concentration; our hearing enables us to make complex calculations about space, texture, weight and quality, which can help us form opinions about where we are or what we're doing. If you close your eyes and click your fingers, you can tell what size and shape the room is, and what materials it is decorated with. Imagine going into the bathroom and doing it, and then a cathedral. You are able to make calculations about spatial dynamics that tell you whether you're in a small tiled room or a large stone one. That information will affect you: you might feel colder or cleaner. If it was soft and dull, you might feel warmer.

Tap on a surface and you'll know what material it is made from. You'll judge how solid or flimsy you think it is, just as you do by the clunk of a car door. There's an entire department at most car manufacturers, normally called something like NVH – 'noise, vibration and harshness' – who make sure things sound well made. If when you close a door you hear a low-pitched and satisfying thud, you'll transfer feelings of solidity, safety and sturdiness to the car, even though it has little to do with the actual performance of the vehicle itself.

That transference of quality will also affect the other senses. A study called 'It's the Sizzle that Sells' (the title referring to a classic 1930s quote from advertising guru

Elmer Wheeler: 'Don't sell the steak, sell the sizzle') showed how the sound made by a coffee machine can make the coffee taste better. In a set-up reminiscent of the 1980s advert for Nescafé, when someone pretends to be a percolator rather than admitting to only having instant coffee, the study served cups of identical coffee, having played different coffee machine sounds from behind a counter. The researcher would say to the volunteer, 'Let me make you a cup of coffee, madam.' And then, from behind the counter would come a weak slurping noise, along with the sound of a thin stream of liquid dripping into a flimsy plastic cup. When the coffee was served, the volunteer would judge its flavour: weak, watery and cheap.

'I'll make you another, shall I?' the researcher might say. And then the volunteer would hear beans grinding, steam pressure, frothing and a steady stream of liquid pouring into a porcelain mug. Then the coffee was served, exactly the same as before. But this time it was rich and full of flavour; the volunteer is willing to pay more for it.

The key is to pay attention to the noises around you – realise how incredible our sense of hearing is and the amazing calculations we're able to process from even the smallest of noises. We use them to form an opinion of our environment and to alter our behaviour. We are used to listening to music, but we don't think about or use sound often enough.

CHAPTER 5

Work

Most days, for most people, include work. It is a necessary element of our lives that is incredibly rewarding for some and mundane for others. Either way, the spaces in which we work can be vastly improved, sensorially speaking.

As the day develops, there are times when you are better off focusing your attention on certain types of activities. We are predisposed to be better at different forms of thinking at different points of the day, as a result once again of the all-powerful circadian rhythm. Broadly speaking, research shows that we're better at things that require focus and attention to detail between 8am and 2pm, peaking at around 11am. The morning is also the best time to get someone to say 'yes' to something. Creativity rules in the latter part of the working day when, as we'll come to later, a little mind wandering and distraction is a good thing. Meetings, brainstorms and 'ideations' are also best in the early afternoon, with 3pm being cited as the perfect time for an internal get-together.

Taking the lead from this temporal flux in our capacities, we will look at what you should be doing and when you should be doing it, before creating sensory prescriptions to help you perform as effectively as possible. Sometimes this might encompass every one of our faculties, while at other times it might single out a solitary sensory enhancement that could give you the edge.

Admittedly, very few of us have total control over our working space or meeting rooms. However, you might possess the freedom of a nomadic worker, able to choose the perfect location to match you goals, whether that's a shared workspace, a café or your kitchen table. Wherever you conduct your business and whatever you do for work, you will gain measurable benefits if you employ even a fraction of the sensory prescriptions that follow.

Where to Work – Your Immediate Environment

Let's assume that it is around 9am and you're just about ready to start work. What are the fundamental considerations you should have in your mind about your surroundings, now that you are beginning to think multisensorially? Maybe you hot-desk in the office and have a few options of where you could sit. You may be getting set up at the kitchen table, or roaming the streets looking for somewhere to work for the day. Before we get into sensory prescriptions for specific tasks, let's look at some overarching factors about where to situate yourself and what your environment should be like.

NATURAL LIGHT

In 2015, the 'Human Spaces Survey' was conducted, asking 7,600 office workers across sixteen countries how they felt about their workplace environments. Forty-seven per cent of respondents reported having no natural light at all. A recurring theme in this book is that exposure to natural light is always of huge benefit, whatever the task at hand. Artificial lighting has its place, but it should ideally be a background enhancement to the real thing rather than the sole source of illumination. Natural light keeps us alert and makes us feel more energised. Prolonged exposure will help align our circadian clock while we work, as well as giving us more chance of a good night's sleep and a better state of mind tomorrow. So if you can, find a nice spot by a window and you'll feel a whole lot better.

PLANTS AND GREENERY

Another constant theme in our day is the presence of plants and greenery, which has a calming, stress-relieving effect on us. For example, a study in a Pennsylvania hospital in the 1970s and 1980s showed that every patient recovering from surgery who was given a room with a view over the park recovered more quickly, needed less medication and was discharged earlier than those patients who had a view of a brick wall. In the Human Space Survey, 58 per cent of office workers said there were no greenery or plants in their workplace.

Being around plants has also been shown to help us maintain our attention for longer. Researchers in Norway gave a group of students a mental arithmetic test to complete in a room with potted plants, while others sat the same test in an empty room. Results were better when there was greenery, and the students' ability to mentally recover improved as well. In the same way that plants help us recover physically, they also help us recover from mental exertion. It's all down to our innate biophilia – the connection that we have to nature. Having a potted plant or two on your desk or choosing a spot to work that has a bit of foliage nearby will improve your mental and physical state, and also help you work better for longer.

TEMPERATURE

Walk into your potential workplace and assess how it feels on your skin. Does it feel a little hot? If you're going to spend a lot of time there, a cosy environment might be good. Is there a chill in the air? Well, that might keep you more alert. A team investigating productivity and mental stamina of office workers ran tests in different atmospheric conditions, and discovered that the perfect temperature for getting things done is 21.6ºC. Below that, people became distracted because they weren't quite comfortable. However, for every 1°C above the perfect temperature there was a 1–2 per cent drop in the subjects' performance. Unless you carry a thermometer around with you, this precise sweet spot will be difficult to gauge. But focus on your senses, and if something's not right, do what you can to change it or go somewhere else. Consider the temperature in the place you're planning on working. The warmer you are, the harder it will be to maintain your focus over the course of a day.

THE HEIGHT OF THE ROOM

When deciding on the right place to work, you might want to consider the height of the ceiling. It seems a strange thought, but instinctively it makes sense. Our mental state is more affected by the space around us than we realise, and the height of the ceiling is cited by psychologists as one of the main architectural details of a space that affects our behaviour. Low ceilings might feel warm and cosy, but they also trigger a feeling of confinement. High ceilings might feel colder and less intimate, but they also make us feel freer. According to some research, people who live in homes with higher ceilings have more energy and better health than those with low ceilings. It's been suggested that children play more quietly and precisely in low-ceilinged spaces, but loudly and with greater imagination when the ceiling is above eight feet high. In adulthood, the effect on our thinking and behaviour is the same. Low ceilings are better for anything requiring focus and attention to detail, while high ceilings are preferable for thinking more openly and imaginatively.

WHAT'S ON YOUR DESK?

What's in front of you while you work can help to encourage different ways of thinking, so what could you bring to work with you that you can pop on the table to make it yours? There's a psychological effect called 'material priming', which centres around the fact that we attach meaning to objects because of what they're used for, what they might represent and because of our personal experience. That meaning will influence our behaviour and affect how we process information, in a similar way to the effects of enclothed cognition we discussed earlier. In one study, a group of college students were shown a picture of a gun and given some hypothetical social situations to respond to. For instance, what would they do if someone insulted a friend of theirs? The responses were a lot more aggressive than those of people who hadn't been 'material primed' by seeing the gun, even though it was just a picture.

A study at Stanford University proved that after people were shown pictures of items that we associate with business – a fountain pen, a briefcase or a boardroom table – they behaved more competitively, were less cooperative and displayed greater self-interest. Subjects were primed with either the business-related images or photos of random nonsensical things like a whale or a toothbrush, before being given a series of tests. One involved completing words where there were a range of correct answers – for example, '_ar' could be 'bar', 'far', 'car' or 'war'. A good one is c__p___tive – cooperative, or competitive? The psychological theory is that the word that you choose is indicative of the thoughts that are currently at the forefront of your mind, revealing your inner feelings. It's quite a fun test to try yourself; see if you're a cut-throat executive or a collaborative creative. In the study, the students consistently opted for the more aggressive words after they had looked at the business-related objects.

The effects of 'material priming' can be used to our advantage. Whatever your focus of work, bring along some paraphernalia that will help to get you in the right mindset. If you need to be brutal and business-like, choose a fountain pen and a Filofax as your notebook and pen. If you want to be gentler in your thinking, use a pencil and a Moleskine notebook. You could take this idea and run with it; a Rubik's Cube might help you problem solve; a calculator could help you be more accurate and exact. You could also use personal items that remind you of a time, place or feeling. As long as there is clear meaning to you, the object will prime you to think and behave in a way that's congruent with that meaning.

A BIT OF VARIETY

Variety is the spice of life, and we should all think about instilling some sensorial variety into our lives. According to a paper reviewing the benefits of better workplace design in 2006, a changing sensory environment keeps the mind active – that might mean slight variations in the lighting throughout the day, an ever-evolving vista or a variety of smells that waft your way every now and again. It's one reason why cafés can be a good place to work, with their low-level buzz of activity and waves of coffee and baking aromas circulating around the space.

Perfect sensorial variety needs to be gentle – drastic changes in the environment or sudden loud noises would be too distracting – but they do have to be noticeable. Being in an unchanging, sensorially devoid environment, people lose focus and creative drive. In an article back in 1968, the behavioural psychologist Robert Cooper wrote that 'an environment devoid of sensory stimulation can lead to boredom and passivity'.

To create sensorial variety in your day, you might sit somewhere different every now and then. Change the things on your desk and sit by a window if you can, for the benefits of natural light and the variations in lighting caused by the changing weather. Drink and eat different things instead of continuous coffees or teas, in order to bring a variety of tastes and aromas to your working day – maybe work your way through a herbal tea variety pack each week. Have something tactile and interesting to touch around you; even one of those squidgy stress balls can give you a moment of sensory indulgence.

If you have many tasks throughout the day, sensorial

variety may come naturally, but a lot of the time you will find yourself stuck in one mode and focusing on one task for the whole day. In those times, it is important to remember to shake it up a little throughout the day, no matter how repetitive the work – you'll feel and perform better for it.

First Thing – Being Productive

The first few hours of the working day are the best time for being productive, getting through any jobs that require attention to detail and tasks that might be repetitive and mundane. Research into people's performance at different times of the day shows a steady decline in things like logical reasoning, speed, accuracy and short-term memory from around 8am onwards. Anything that might require you to think straight and remember lots of small things is apparently not worth bothering about after 2pm. In 1975, the experimental psychologist Simon Folkard made some seminal discoveries in this field, building on work that had been conducted since the early 1960s. Folkard mapped the decline in our abilities throughout the day by getting students to take a variety of tests, starting at 8am and then every three hours until 11pm. People's speed at completing the tasks got gradually faster until 2pm, and dropped off dramatically thereafter. However, accuracy – the amount of answers they were getting right – got steadily got worse from 8am onwards. The subjects' body temperatures – a function that's linked to our internal body clocks and the circadian rhythm – were also measured at each of the test times. As the day goes on, our body temperature rises, and as the people in the study got warmer, their short-term memory and logical reasoning scores got worse. Evidently we are predisposed to complete mundane, repetitive jobs that require focus and accuracy, tick off lists and check emails first thing in the day.

The first sensory prescription we need to look at, then, is one that has to do with this mindset – to further enhance our productivity and focus, and to help our ability to complete repetitive jobs with accuracy. Beyond this optimal morning time, you can use these insights to create a focus-enhancing atmosphere whatever the time of day, and whenever you require attention to detail and accuracy.

SURROUND YOURSELF BY THE COLOUR RED

Having control over the colours of the walls in your working environment isn't always an option, but if you are able to choose a place to sit when you want to be productive, pick a place with red walls. The colour red has a stimulating effect – it makes us more alert and speeds up our heart rate. Scientists from Vancouver looked at how this inbuilt reaction to red affects how careful we are when working on something that requires accuracy. They asked groups to complete a variety of tasks on computers that had different coloured screens, which cast coloured light on their workspace. When the participants were bathed in red light, they showed greater attention to detail and were better at tasks that tested their cognitive abilities; conversely, their abstract reasoning and creativity improved when the screens were blue (more on that later).

People make more typing errors when they're in a white room compared to a red room, which is interesting because most office spaces are white. Red is the most stimulating colour, but other bright and warm colours such as orange and zesty yellow have a similar effect. You might even bedeck the place with bright art or pictures. At the risk of sounding like a Californian yoga instructor, you need to create an environment with good energy. But I mean that in the neurologically and physiologically measurable sense, and not the 'far-out' way.

You don't have to be entirely surrounded by red and bright colour – for most of us, finding such a space is a bit of a big ask. But like the study that just used a red-coloured screen, find a way to bring red into your vicinity. You might use a red notepad when you're doing this kind of work and put it on the desk in front of you – as long as it's in your field of vision, it will have some kind of effect.

BRIGHT LIGHT

Similar to bright colours, we are more accurate and productive in brighter lighting. Early morning is a good time of the day to get a serious blast of light – turn on every light and sit by a window if you can, letting the natural light wash over you. One conclusive study in this field was conducted in Guildford, a haven for uninspiring working environments and repetitive office jobs. The researchers took over two floors of an office building and set them to different lighting conditions for four weeks at a time. When the lights were at a whopping 17,000K of 'blue-enriched white light', the people in the offices showed better performance, concentration and alertness and an improvement in their general mood. They also slept better at night, felt better the following day and were reportedly increasingly more 'up for it'.

CINNAMON SCENT, TEA OR BUN

As ever in the sensory world, congruence is key, and we shall begin to see the pieces fall into place. Firstly, a stimulating scent helps productivity in the same way as a stimulating colour. Across studies that look at focus in a work environment or maintaining the attention of consumers as they walk around a shop, bright and fresh scents like peppermint, citrus and cinnamon have been proven to work well. In a Japanese office, the smell of citrus in the air was reported to increase typing speed and accuracy by 50 per cent. One study from Wheeling University in West Virginia involved not only filling a room with scent, but also getting participants to chew flavoured chewing gum. When people chewed cinnamon gum, they showed an improvement in problem-solving and short-term memory.

When we look at how scent and colour work together,

we see a super-additive, accumulative effect in terms of improvements to mood and task performance. The best combination for accuracy and productivity is a stimulating red-coloured room, and a stimulating scent – cinnamon being the aroma of choice.

Cinnamon has proven positive effects, and it is also linked to the colour red in our multisensory, synaesthetic minds. Dig some out of your spice cupboard and have a sniff, thinking about what colour the smell is. I'd hope that you would say it smells somewhere in the red and warm side of the colour spectrum. Of course, the powder is a reddish brown. It's related to Christmas for a lot of people, and so is linked to the Christmas colour palette. And it has a sweet and warm smell and taste – both of which are instinctually red-ish.

The genius of the West Virginia chewing gum study shows that we don't have to bring an atomiser bottle of cinnamon essential oil to work with us, enforcing our sensory prescription on people around us. Instead you could drink a cinnamon herbal tea to fill your immediate environment with the aroma. Or you might want to snack on a cinnamon bun.

MUSIC THAT MAKES YOU HAPPY, AND A NICE HUBBUB SOUND

The use of music to accompany work is a contentious subject. As recently as 2019, an experiment asked over 200 participants to attempt different creative and problem-solving tasks while listening to instrumental music, music with lyrics and music with foreign lyrics. The results showed that whichever music was playing made no difference at all; the presence of a hubbub of activity in the background produced the best results. The constant bustle of chatter and movement in a busy café is a perfect backdrop for the kind of focus and attention you want in the morning.

A study in Minnesota showed that high school students were worse at reading and comprehension when listening to chart music. The main factor cited was the music's simple and catchy lyrics – categorical proof that the whimsical pop stylings of Taylor Swift can be bad for your brain. On the instrumental side of things, Mozart's name is mentioned a lot, with his music often heralded as having some kind of magical power to enhance brain function. In 1993, three scientists named Frances Rauscher, Gordon Shaw and Catherine Ky coined the now-famous term 'The Mozart Effect'. This began as a proven insight that the Master's music impacts our spatial reasoning, before being hijacked to refer to the generalisation that all classical music makes you smarter, especially if you are exposed to it at a young age.

If you like the music that is playing and are familiar with it, it's likely to put you in a better mood – and this has a measurable impact on many forms of work performance, especially when the task at hand is monotonous. If the music is unusual, it will demand too much of your attention. In Sweden a group of scientists got twenty-four students to concentrate on reading in different sound and music conditions: silence, a café atmosphere, listening to music they liked and listening to music they did not like. Their focus and attention was worst with music they didn't like, and best with music they liked or the café atmosphere.

Your accompanying music for morning productivity should fit the other sensory elements, and stimulating smells, lighting and colours naturally go with stimulating sound and music. So the ideal choices are upbeat music that you know well, a nice hubbub of activity or a mix of both.

SOLID TABLE AND UPRIGHT CHAIR – NO SLOUCHING

The chair you sit in will affect how you behave and think. We're more inflexible in our thinking if we sit in a hard rather than a soft chair, but we'll also be more logical and direct and show more self-belief. At Ohio State University, the psychology professor Richard Petty showed that we are more confident in our own work when we sit upright and show more doubt when we slouch. He convinced a group of students that they were taking part in a job interview and asked them to maintain different postures while writing about their capabilities to fill a particular role. When they were sitting upright they did themselves proud, writing in complete confidence about their own abilities. But when they were slouched over the table, they showed little belief in their skills and undersold themselves.

OTHER THINGS – GRID PAPER, BIRO, A LAB COAT PERHAPS?

The ultimate sensorial environment is all but achieved, with the senses working together to make you faster, more accurate and more alert. But there is still place for other enhancements. Firstly, we should consider material priming. What objects will help with these types of tasks? A calculator or Filofax to help with business acumen and precision? And a geometry set from school, perhaps. You should keep a different notepad for different tasks, and the one for this morning's jobs should be squared or at least ruled paper, rather than blank, the structure of the grid helping focus your mind and promote more precise thought. A biro or ballpoint pen would be best, due to their functional connotations; pencils are creative and fountain pens are prone to smudging in a way that is counterintuitive to the precision that is required.

The definitive study into enclothed cognition by Adam and Galinsky that we came across in the morning showed that individuals were better at maths and problem-solving when they were wearing a lab coat. You will probably not want to wear such a thing in the office or in a café, but surely you can at home, where no one's watching? The rules of enclothed cognition and material priming dictate that if you assign a meaning to an item, your mind and behaviour will follow. So without going the whole hog, you could bring something to the table that you either already attribute meaning to or can build up a new association with. With every element of any sensory prescription, the more you use them, the more you will reinforce sensory memories, emotions and associations.

A SENSORY PRESCRIPTION FOR PRODUCTIVITY, FOCUS AND ATTENTION TO DETAIL

- **Colour** – Bright red. Choose a red room, or at least get a bright red notepad.
- **Lighting** – Bright, blueish white. Natural light.
- **Scent and taste** – Cinnamon. Spritz a cinnamon scent or get a desktop diffuser. Otherwise, drink cinnamon tea, chew cinnamon gum or eat a cinnamon bun.
- **Music and sound** – Upbeat and lively music that you like, preferably without lyrics. Otherwise a steady hubbub.
- **Furniture** – A rigid and upright table and chair.
- **Other things** – Items related to productivity, such as a calculator and ruler. Use a biro or ballpoint pen. Wear a lab coat or something related to organisational thought, such as a watch or glasses.

Mid-Morning – Selling Yourself and Your Ideas

The morning is the best time of the day to present your work or sell yourself. We're generally in a more positive mood in the first half of the day, so it's a good time of day for anything where the goal is to get someone to make a positive decision in your favour. When two researchers, Scott Golder and Michael Macy, analysed around 508 million Twitter posts from across the world, looking at people's mood states by picking up on the frequency of positive and negative words, they found that people write more positive things in the morning and at weekends.

As the day progresses, we all fall prey to 'decision fatigue', the consequences of which can be life-changing. In a review of over a thousand court cases, a group of business professors from Stanford University and Ben-Gurion University of the Negev, Israel, revealed that incarcerated defendants were 70 per cent more likely to receive parole when they appeared before the judge in the morning. When two people had committed the same crime and served the same amount of time in jail but were facing the judge at different times (8.50am and 4.25pm respectively), the one who was seen earlier was let off and the other one wasn't. If you ever find yourself in trouble with the law, ask your lawyer if they can get you a morning court hearing.

This idea of mental tiredness was pioneered by a psychologist called Roy Baumeister, who conducted a series of experiments that showed that we have a finite resource for decision-based things like self-control. What he called 'ego depletion' suggested that willpower can run out, like a muscle that gets tired the more we use it. In a similar experiment years later, inspired by the onslaught of decisions involved in planning her own wedding, Professor Jean Twenge investigated whether having to make any type of choice again and again would exhaust our mental reserves. She found that it did, and the concept of 'decision fatigue' was born. As it sets in, we become mentally depleted and stop wanting to weigh up options – we just go for the simplest default option. If we are presented with something that is new or in any way challenging, 'no' will by far be the least mentally strenuous answer.

The morning, before decision fatigue has set in, is the best time to pitch an idea and sell a product, service or yourself. Let's look at the best sensory tips to make yourself more persuasive, and the sensory prescription to get the recipient of your pitch to say 'yes'.

LISTEN TO BASSY MUSIC

We've all heard of power-hungry businessmen shouting at themselves in the bathroom mirror before a boardroom battle. If that feels too aggressive, what about putting on a bit of music? Listening to bass-heavy tunes before you go and sell your ideas has been shown to make your arguments more forceful and your presence more impactful. In one piece of research, people on a university debating team were given different musical playlists to listen to before they stepped onto a podium and argued the case for things that had been chosen to be particularly unemotional. Some members of the team listened to classical music, others drum and bass, and others had silence. In almost every case, the person who had listened to the drum and bass music before taking to the stage argued most effectively.

SPEAK LOW

The sound of your voice is an important indicator of confidence. According to a study where people's brain responses were measured in real time, we judge how confident a person is within 200 milliseconds of hearing them speak. We are more likely to believe a person who has a low-pitched voice, whether they are male or female – low pitch communicates power and strength, wherever you find it. Animals will lower the pitch of their roars to appear more dominant. A lower pitch conveys larger size and heavy weight, qualities which also communicate power and strength. You should also try to speak relatively quickly. A languid drawl won't help you, but small bursts of fast talking give off an air of confidence.

STAND TALL AND WIDE

Your posture will affect your own feelings of confidence. Studies into 'embodied cognition' show how affecting certain stances and even facial expressions can change how you feel and behave. In 1988, a group showed that when we artificially make ourselves smile, we immediately find things more enjoyable. By holding our heads high, we instil feelings of self-pride. As we've already seen, a study that got people to either sit upright or slouch resulted in them feeling more confident or unsure of their own abilities respectively. By assuming a power pose, we will make ourselves look and feel more confident, powerful and dominant.

And if you're going to go full-on gorilla, it is probably best to get it out of the way in the privacy of a bathroom like the manly stockbrokers, rather than in front of your prospective client, employer or judge. And as with your tone and tempo of speech, embodied cognition also works if you're making a sales pitch over the phone, so smile and sit up straight; the person at the other end of the line will be able to tell.

WEAR BLACK

As we discovered when getting dressed, black is seen as the most confident colour, closely followed by red (though the latter colour is also seen as arrogant). If you haven't dressed appropriately, maybe either slip on something black or add an accessory that can boost your confidence through the same enclothed effect. Also returning to what we learned earlier, wearing a Superman T-shirt underneath your top would give yourself an edge.

Once you are feeling confident, powerful and raring to go, the goal is to get yourself in a positive mood: calm, relaxed, content and maybe a little excited. You want to encourage what psychologists call 'approach behaviour': being open to new things and ideas. This may be only slightly relevant if you are sharing some financial figures, but it will be of huge importance if you're pitching creative concepts or a new product.

From the point of view of a sensory prescription, being positive, calm and 'open' come together quite nicely, though there are a few nuanced choices to be made depending on what it is you're trying to get your audience to agree to.

GREEN MEANS GO

Colours that are on the cooler end of the spectrum get the best results when persuading people to hand over money. A famous study by Joseph Bellizzi and Robert Hite from Arizona State and Kansas State universities in 1992 set up simulated red and blue shopping environments and found that people in the blue shop browsed more products, made decisions more quickly and made more purchases overall.

But blue isn't the only cool colour on the spectrum; the colour to turn to when it comes to being persuasive is green. We already know that green has many psychological benefits. Having plants in a shop increases sales, as well as the amount of time customers browse for and how much they talk to staff. In a huge study into the colour of offices, 675 people who performed tasks in different-coloured rooms preferred the one that was green. While workers' accuracy and speed improved in the red office, people liked being in the green room most.

In one survey into the relationships between colour and emotions, 95.9 per cent of people listed green as the most positive colour. It is also cited by colour therapists and psychologists as encouraging generosity and sincerity. One study from 1964 showed that green had a 'facilitating effect' on people's judgements when they were given hypothetical scenarios to react to. Semantically speaking, green means go – it's a welcome rather than a warning. In physiological terms, green-coloured light has a calming, restorative and refreshing effect, which makes it the perfect colour to combat decision fatigue.

However, it's important to note that, as with any colour, green has negative connotations. Shades at the yellowy end of the range are related to sickness and nausea – the green you use should be pure and lush. Also, despite the phrase 'getting the green light', I wouldn't recommend using green lighting – it casts an unappealing hue over everything it touches. Instead, if you aren't able to paint the whole room, bring in greenery with potted plants, present drinks on a green tray and hand out notes in green folders or even on green paper. A study into the influences on voting in elections found that men were more likely to vote for candidates whose positions were printed on green ballot paper.

Include green in your PowerPoint slides when you are presenting the big idea or going for the big sell. If you're having a less formal meeting, choose somewhere surrounded by greenery and use a green notebook, placed prominently on the table. Try to ensure that there's a block of this positive, calming colour in your target's field of vision, and then back it up with a similarly positive scent.

CLEAN CITRUS AROMA

As we explored earlier, wearing a perfume can change your own body language, making others see you as more confident. But beyond affecting your own behaviour, aroma can also play a huge role in winning over the other people in the room.

There are two ways you can play it. The first is to follow the sensory prescription. Positivity is a bright and zesty emotion and so are citrus scents, which also have a strongly positive effect on the type of behaviours we want to encourage in a perfect pitching environment. As well as feeling energetic, citrus is also calming – an aroma compound called D-limonene, found in the skin of citrus fruit, is proven to slow the heart rate and reduce feelings of stress and anxiety.

Citrus aromas inspire the 'approach behaviours' that I mentioned before – being open to new things and showing more explorative thinking. In one study, researchers rigged up scent machines with either lavender or grapefruit in a shop and tracked the movements of thirty randomly selected customers. When there was grapefruit in the air, the shoppers explored more products and made more impulse purchases; when asked how they felt as they left the store, they were in a better mood.

Rooms that smell 'clean' have a very interesting effect on people's charitable nature, which is a sort of moral equivalent to being clean. A research group in Toronto gave ninety-nine students a folder containing various written tasks, with the instruction that they had to complete them in either a neutral-smelling room or one that had been sprayed with citrus-scented Windex. Included in the folder was a flyer for Habitat for Humanity, a charity that was looking for volunteers and donations. Twenty-two per cent of people in the Windex room pledged donations, compared to six per cent in the non-scented room.

So citrus is a winner, and lime would be the one – it links with the colour green, with the two elements working together to make the green greener and the lime more citrusy. Citrus smells are positive and bright but also calming; they open people up to new ideas and can also help to loosen the wallets of anyone within sniffing distance. It's easy to introduce lime aroma into any environment, whether you are in a meeting room or café. Put fresh lime in the glasses of water you hand out, spritz a little in the air or wipe the table with a lime-scented cleaner before your meeting.

A second approach to scent is to use an aroma that reflects the service or product that you're trying to sell. Research into the use of smells in shops shows that if an aroma is congruent with a product category – like the smell of baking around the bread in a supermarket – sales will increase. More 'experience-based' smells can be used as a kind of storytelling device, making pitches more immersive. Think about how different showing someone a holiday photograph is from what the experience was actually like – a snap of the beach might look nice enough, but it's flat compared to the actual experience. If they could smell the sun cream and hear the waves, they'd be able to imagine themselves there. If you were selling this holiday to them, how much more enticing would it be if you engaged all their senses? Going back to Antonio Damasio from the Introduction, 'we are feeling machines that think'. By engaging the most emotional sense – smell – you can turn a rational decision into an emotional one.

If your service, concept or product has an obvious olfactory accompaniment, it's worth using a spritz of something to bring it to life. This might seem a bit baffling if you're selling financial services, but try and think about something like that in a lateral way. What's the emotion you're selling in that situation? Maybe it's trust. What's the smell of trust? If you're British, it might be tea or baking – things you associate with warmth. There will always be a feeling that you can evoke with a scent – identify it and it will help you no end.

QUALITY SOUND

When we think about sound for a sales pitch, there is the obvious fact that you mostly just want people to listen to your voice, so a musical accompaniment isn't appropriate. The important thing though, is the *quality* of sound that people experience. So much of how we feel about the world around us is coloured by what we hear. As we explored in the section on hearing, the solid clunk of a car door makes you believe that the vehicle is well made. A bright and reflective room feels colder than a soft, muted one. And as I said before, a low-pitched voice makes you think a person is more competent.

I once conducted a sensory audit of Bentley's flagship

showroom in Berkeley Square in London's Mayfair. It's a huge tiled space, with a double-height ceiling and a selection of cars costing £200,000 and above, all displayed like works of art. The impression they were looking to achieve was of premium quality, craftsmanship, engineering prowess and status, but sales were not good.

One of the things I brought to their attention was the sound in their showroom. Music was emanating from a tiny transistor radio on the mezzanine floor. The selection? BBC Radio 2. The tinny pop music bounced brightly around the tiled space – it was like listening to music on your phone, in a bathroom. The sound communicated anything but power and quality. What they should have had is something super high fidelity – full and lush, with plenty of bass to reflect the quality of the cars and the feeling you'd get from owning a Bentley.

Similarly, if you're on a conference call and the voices on the other end sound distant, echoey and tinny, it is unlikely that you will trust the ability of the people you're talking to as much as you would if the sound was clear, full and rich. A meeting room in which you present your wares shouldn't sound echoey and cold. Choose a space wisely and think about the sound. Beyond the acoustics of a space, take a moment to listen. Is there a rattling air conditioning unit? A buzzing speaker? Are building works going on outside? All this will contribute to a less relaxed potential client. The aim is for soft, dull, warm sound with little distraction, so you can be heard clearly.

MAKE EVERYTHING FEEL WARM

'A warm personality'. 'A cold reception'. As I mentioned when we looked at the issue of morning fragrance, the most powerful words that affect how we feel about people are 'warm' and 'cold'. The emotion is conveyed through all our senses, but perhaps most powerfully through touch. In 2008, John Bargh from Yale University, a leader in the research of touch, and Lawrence Williams, an associate professor of marketing from the University of Colorado Boulder, conducted a study to show that the physical sensation of warmth translated directly to an emotional feeling of warmth.

As participants were walking into a room to participate in the study, they were met at the door by a man who asked them to hold his drink while he tied his shoelace. Half the time it was a warm coffee and half the time it was iced coffee. When asked afterwards 'What did you think of the person you met outside the room?' the participants overwhelmingly described the person as being either warm or cold, in exact correspondence with the temperature of the drink they had held. Even using those exact words in their descriptions of him, saying 'He was really cold and aloof.' Or 'What a nice, warm person.'

To come across as a warm person is of great personal advantage, so always make sure that you have warm hands before you shake someone else's. As in the study, bring a warm drink for the person you're meeting. And if you hand them something to look at, make sure it feels warm, like a portfolio bound in leather or card rather than cold plastic. If you give people that tactile sense of warmth, they will feel warmer towards you.

SOFT TEXTURES AND HEAVY WEIGHT

As well as warmth, there are other 'haptic', or touch-related, qualities that are directly translated into emotions. John Bargh, from the 'warm drink' experiment above, conducted a host of studies with Joshua Ackerman, another master of touch, into the ways that people's judgements change when they are touching or holding different weighted and textured objects. Forty-eight people were handed either light or heavy clipboards and asked to fill out a survey about how much government funding should be allocated to various social services. People gave more money when they were holding the heavier clipboards. Men were particularly affected, because the weight translates to a kind of bravado that made them splash the cash. Equally, if you hand someone the resumé of a job interviewee on a heavy clipboard, they'll rate the applicant as more competent and a better fit for the job than when they are given the same information on a light clipboard.

The researchers also tested the difference between the texture of chairs. They sat ninety-eight participants in soft, cushioned or hard, wooden chairs and got them to enter into a negotiation task around buying a second-hand car. People in the rigid chair were less willing to shift their position and increase their price; when the people in the comfy chair were asked to make a second offer on the car, they increased their amount willingly.

So whatever you hand out, make sure it's weighty and has a nice, soft – and warm – texture. This might be the paper you print on or the folder you use for a report. If you have a soft chair to hand, let your guest sit in it and they'll be more generous to you. And definitely make sure that they are sitting – no standing-up sales pitches or negotiations. A study by the sensory marketeer Luca Cian asked a group of students a series of tempting questions while they were either sitting or standing – conundrums such as 'Would you be willing to sneak out to a concert when you still have homework to do?' While they were standing up, the subjects exercised good self-control, but when they were sitting down when the question was posed, they were straight out of the window, band T-shirt on and concert ticket in hand.

SHARP SHAPES

The final element of the sensory prescription is shape. If we follow the multisensorial flow from aroma – bright and zesty lime – then we instinctually consider angular shapes. Angularity, as we explored when we were discussing exercise, feels active and positive. In her book about decoding design, the branding guru Maggie Macnab refers to triangles as being symbolic of aspiration and inspiration. She talks about a mountain's peak as being a metaphor for inspiration.

Shape can come in the form of something visual, as in a logo or graphic on a slide you're presenting, and it also crosses over into touch. Holding something with more angularity to it can make the person presenting come across as sharp and dynamic, in the same way that holding something solid and heavy translates to feelings of competence and quality. An angular glass will also make the lime in the water taste zestier and more refreshing. Your client will think, 'Damn, this water's good' and marvel at the quality of your refreshments.

TALK ABOUT THE SENSES

To back up all this sensorial immersion, whenever you are pitching or selling something and there is the opportunity to do so, prompt your audience to engage their senses by thinking about them. Engaging and focusing on the senses is used in many forms of therapy and mindfulness to bring people into the moment, but research also shows that when people are asked to *imagine* touching, tasting or smelling something, it engages the same parts of their brain as when they actually do it.

When we pick something up in a shop, we start to fall prey to what's called 'the endowment effect', meaning that we feel like we already own it and consequently find it harder to leave the shop without it. One study proved that even imagining you've touched something can cause the endowment effect. And another piece of research showed that when people were shown a picture of chocolate chip cookies and asked to imagine the smell, they began to salivate. So whatever you're pitching, refer to the senses. Ask people to imagine a smell, a sound, the feeling of picking something up or even an emotion and they'll be more present and engaged.

A SENSORY PRESCRIPTION FOR CONFIDENCE, COMPETENCE AND GETTING OTHERS TO SAY 'YES'

For you:

- Listen to bassy music before you go into a meeting or make a phone call.
- Speak low and in relatively quick bursts.
- Stand strong and smile, even if you're on the phone.
- Wear black, in order to come across as confident and intelligent.

For the prospective client:

- **Colour** – Green, but not a sickly yellowish shade. Think lush grass, or a darker British racing green. Have a green notepad or a green background on a PowerPoint slide. Choose a location with lots of greenery around, or have potted plants in the room.
- **Scent and taste** – Lime, or other 'clean' citrus. Serve water with ice and lime, spritz the room with lime or clean the table with the scent, to encourage some charitable generosity. Or sell with smell – use a scent that reflects what you're selling, to bring your presentation to life and make it more emotional.

- **Sound** – Muted, dull and matte. Avoid rooms with tinny echo or any distracting noise, such as rattling air-con, buzzing or building works.
- **Temperature** – Warm. Have warm hands, use warm materials – try to avoid plastic and other synthetics, as they feel emotionally cold.
- **Texture** – Soft and weighty. Hand your guest a solid folder and use weighty paper. Sit people in soft, padded chairs.
- **Shape** – Angular. Serve the lime-infused water in angular glasses. Maybe make the graphics in your presentation more angular, so they seem more active, dynamic and positive.
- **Language** – Talk about the senses. Ask them to imagine touching, holding, smelling and hearing. Whatever might be relevant. And even if it isn't – use sensorially evocative language to get them to focus on their own senses, bringing them into the moment and triggering the emotional parts of the brain.

Lunchtime – The Power of Planning a Treat for Later

As the day goes on and you can feel the hours ahead looming into the distance, it's a good time to make a plan for something rewarding later on, to make it worthwhile. A glass of wine, a leisurely cycle, or you might plan to buy some lovely ingredients and make a nice meal – whatever gets you excited. Apart from signalling the end of the working day when it arrives, it's the looking forward to something that is what I really want you to experience.

Waiting before you get to enjoy something not only increases how much you like it, but the waiting part can be just as good as the thing itself. It's a kind of delayed gratification that I use when I devise what are called 'consumption rituals' for brands and products. A good example is having to wait 119.53 seconds to sip a pint of Guinness (that's the official exact time), while it swirls and settles into two distinct layers before receiving a final top-up from the bartender. Research shows that the pint will taste better because of that time spent building up expectation.

This idea of delayed gratification is also the reason that I have at times helped brands design slightly overcomplicated or unnecessarily hard-to-open packaging, postponing the big reveal. One study of crisp packets showed that when the packaging was harder to open, people said the crisps were tastier. If you feel like you've had to put some effort in, your treat at the end will be all the sweeter. Also, as I said, the wait might actually be better. In 2002, scientists used fMRI scanners to measure people's brain responses while they waited for a sweet treat and then ate it. The scans showed that their levels of dopamine – the pleasure signal in the brain – were just as high during their anticipation of the treat as when they were eating it. Planning a treat will get your pleasure juices flowing, putting you in a more positive mood. Throughout the day, when things start to

WORK

get on top of you and weigh you down, thinking about the treat will alleviate the pain a little.

Early Afternoon – Better Collaboration and Teamwork

The early afternoon is a good time for an internal meeting – 3pm on a Tuesday is cited as the best time. Apparently, that's when most people have the least work to do.

Meetings with fellow employees, other companies or agencies aren't necessarily about a hard sell; their purpose is to set the stage for collaboration – a 'chemistry meeting', in the corporate parlance of our times. Quite often they are a little dry to begin with, especially if it's a room of strangers. There can be paranoia about power and struggles around roles and responsibilities, or the lack of chatter as you file into a room might just be a result of a bit of social timidity. However, with a few sensory enhancements that encourage openness, social interaction and collaboration, you can get people talking, ensuring that everyone works together and diffusing any worries into the (floral-scented) air.

FRESH FLOWERS

In a conference room in Las Vegas in 2008, a group of people working in the gambling industry met as a focus group to discuss a new slot machine. The room was lightly scented with geraniums. Next door, in a virtually identical conference room, a similar group had gathered to discuss the same machine, but their room didn't smell of anything. As they would discover soon after, there was no new slot machine – the people were unwitting subjects of an experiment staged by two researchers from Cornell University, Dina Zemke and Stowe Shoemaker, to test the effects of aroma on how they bonded and interacted. In both rooms the people were left to their own devices for fifteen minutes, having been told that the moderator was running late. In the geranium-scented room, there was more social cohesion than in the non-scented room, signified by eye contact, conversation, open body language and physical contact.

A few different studies have shown that floral scents cause people to interact more and break down social barriers. Another study, with quite a bizarre premise, had people stand and watch a mime act, before asking them to step forward and position the mime to reflect a certain emotion. People were three times more likely to go ahead and touch the mime when there was a simple floral scent in the air, than when other fragrances, such as Chanel No. 5 or baby powder, were used.

Lavender has also been shown to increase feelings of trust; generally, floral scents get people talking, interacting and behaving more openly. It could be because they're relaxing, so people are less stressed and standoffish, or maybe all it takes is the presence of a pleasant odour. But floral scents do have a greater effect than other nice smells, so fill your meeting room with flowers and spray a bit of lavender or geranium into the air before your collaborative session. However, be careful that your meeting room doesn't start smelling like an old lady's house – the scent should be fresh, and also natural. Any hint of syntheticness will have a detrimental effect.

YELLOW

While red helps you keep alert and green promotes positive decisions, when you want people to feel upbeat, positive and optimistic, the optimal colour is yellow. It's far less aggressive than red, but is still lively. Studies using fMRI scans have shown that yellow light waves stimulate brain wave activity and trigger 'rational alertness'. The renowned colour therapist Suzy Chiazzari lists happiness, optimism and rational stimulation as effects of being around yellow. In the survey I mentioned earlier that listed green as the most positive colour (with 95.9 per cent of people agreeing), yellow came a close second, with 93.5 per cent.

Yellow links nicely to the scent of flowers, being associated with the sun and summer. A group of researchers in Taiwan reviewed all the colour theories in history and found that yellow has always been seen as positive. As for negative connotations, the only ones that came up are fear, cowardice and sickness, and if you use a nice sunny yellow I doubt that's how it will come across. If you are hosting this get-together and can't get everyone in a yellow room or use a yellow table, there are other things you can do: fill the room with yellow flowers or hand out agendas in yellow folders. Have a yellow opening slide in your presentation, or make the lights a warm yellow shade.

LOW LIGHTING

In our aim for group cohesion, turning the lights down slightly has been proven to get people acting more socially, most likely because we lower our inhibitions when we feel less 'on show'. Shigeo Kobayashi, a professor of environmental research at Tokyo City University, observed people's behaviour under various lighting conditions, in laboratory settings and in open-air public spaces. He showed that in lower lighting, people sit closer together, adjust their seating position to face each other and lean in to talk. They display more eye contact and other social gestures and talk to each other more. Another study, this time in the UK, got strangers to watch TV together for ten minutes in rooms with either dimmed lighting, bright shelf lights or overhead lights. The brighter the lighting, the more time was spent in silence. The subjects chatted away about what they were watching much more in the low lighting condition. The study also showed that people's feelings of alertness were the same whether the lights were dimmed or bright and overhead. This is good to know, because we want people to interact but also for the room to have a good level of energy.

SOFT TEXTURES

When it comes to texture, John Bargh's research into the effect of touch on the ways we interact is hugely helpful. Of course, heavy items, soft chairs and warm textures are all relevant to this situation too; anything to make people feel more emotional warmth will help collaboration. But one other study of Bargh's has a particular relevance to how we can help people work together. In it, he got groups of people to complete a jigsaw. Some of them had a puzzle with a soft texture on the back of each piece, while others had pieces with sandpaper on the back. The groups with the sandpaper jigsaws judged that their counterparts were less friendly and cooperative than those who were working with the smooth-textured jigsaw, and they also took longer to complete the puzzle.

With anything you hand out, try to use soft textures. For sensory congruence, if you can match the soft feel of flower petals, the super-additive effect will really start to come into play. If this is a group meeting and you are circulating some form of agenda, print it on paper that has a soft texture. You could also place soft placemats in front of every seat or give people soft coasters for their drinks.

Carry this idea to every aspect of texture in the meeting – don't hand out crunchy crisps or nuts, but instead get something that has a soft mouthfeel and doesn't make an abrasive sound – marshmallows, perhaps.

LOW BACKGROUND 'WALLA WALLA'

Silence is deafening and certainly doesn't encourage people to talk. Think about how self-conscious you feel talking in the hushed atmosphere of a gallery or bank, when you find yourself whispering for fear of standing out. If an atmosphere is too loud, it's almost as bad. For one, you can't hear what other people are saying, which undermines the whole point of having a meeting. If you can get the sound level somewhere in the middle, with a nice level of gentle background sound, everyone in the room will feel able to talk. The perfect sound to encourage conversation is referred to as 'walla walla', the murmur of indistinguishable human chatter.

A few years ago I ran a trial for the high street bank TSB in a 'mock shop', where they measured customer reactions to new designs or promotions. We added the gentle murmur of voices and the occasional chink of a teacup through hidden speakers, in order to make people feel more relaxed and comfortable. It's amazing how much of a difference it made; by raising the sound a little so that there wasn't any silence, we found that people instinctively talked more. When we asked them afterwards, not a single person had noticed the added sound.

There are quite a few 'walla walla' sounds on various music streaming services, if you want to try them out. I've also put a selection of my own on the *Sense* website.

GENTLE MUSIC

In a meeting like this, it wouldn't be out of the question to have some gentle music in the background – we know it puts people in a good mood. Slow-tempo background music in shops can make people browse for up to 76 per cent longer. Research into music in restaurants shows that playing slow music makes people take more time over their meal and spend more money.

You need to mirror the sensory qualities around you in the type of music that you play; the sound should be soft and warm, with nothing abrasive like crunchy distorted guitars, and nothing that's cold and digital. As with sound, set the music at a low enough volume that it can sit nicely in the background, noticeable but not intrusive.

SIT AT A ROUND TABLE

King Arthur apparently got it right when he sat his knights around a round table. According to one version of the story, he did it 'to prevent quarrels among his barons, none of whom would accept a lower place than the others'. With a round table rather than a rectangular one, no one is sat at the head, which implies that everyone around it is equal. In the twentieth century, the British psychiatrist Humphry Osmond gave the concept a scientific term – 'sociopetal seating' – and its positive effects were validated. Sitting and facing inwards towards everyone else encourages feelings of openness and promotes conversation. A study on seating arrangements in Japanese classrooms proved that circular seating instilled a greater sense of belonging between classmates and had a positive effect on the students' learning.

GO PARTYING TOGETHER

If there's a particularly difficult atmosphere in a group and you need to create a sense of cohesion, then you should get tribal – and wasted. In a small group, everyone exhibits their own individuality, but this dynamic changes when your small group becomes one group among many. According to a concept called 'self-categorisation theory', how people identify as part of a group depends on the social situation they find themselves in. Consumer research into people's drinking behaviour in the course of a night out – research that I was privy to while working with a brand of tequila-fuelled beer – shows that this change from individuality to tribal togetherness kicks in when a small group moves from having drinks at a friend's flat or pints at a pub to a club. They transition from a group of people each celebrating their own qualities, to a tribe among other tribes, and feelings of trust and support between the members of the group go through the roof.

A SENSORY PRESCRIPTION FOR SOCIAL INTERACTION, CONVERSATION AND WORKING TOGETHER

- **Scent** – Fresh flowers. Gardenia, rose and other floral notes have been shown to get people talking more, and orange blossom is a lovely floral scent that doesn't smell too granny-ish.

- **Colour** – Yellow is bright and optimistic, so choose yellow flowers or have a yellow slide on the screen as people gather. Hand out the agenda in a yellow sleeve.
- **Lighting** – Dim. Turn the lights down to get people out of their shells. And if you can control the colour of the lights, make them a warm yellow.
- **Texture** – Soft, to promote collaboration and social coherence, but don't forget that things should be warm and solid. If you can choose paper that has a soft texture, do.
- **Taste** – Serve soft foods that don't make harsh and crunchy sounds. Marshmallows, sandwiches and cakes are good examples.
- **Sound** – The murmur of voices. Put on a 'walla walla' sound to get people talking.
- **Music** – Some quiet down-tempo music will fill any silence and make a place nicer to be in.
- **Seating** – A circular table with everyone facing inwards helps with social cohesion and openness.
- **Go partying** – If all else fails and you need to encourage group cohesion in a bunch of disparate individuals, go clubbing with them.

Mid-Afternoon – Being Creative

Creativity shouldn't be solely considered the domain of writers, painters or inventors. We are all creative, and getting our creative juices flowing is as important in writing a presentation as it is when you are penning an opus for the stage. Whether you're putting a new business plan together or thinking about a new colour scheme for your lounge, you will find yourself thinking differently, problem-solving and making connections more easily if you bring out your creative side. And to do so means paying attention (but not too much) to the sensory world around you.

'Beauty naturally appears in works unconsciously created.' The Japanese philosopher Soetsu Yanagi wrote this lovely sentence, itself a thing of beauty, in his essay *The Beauty of Miscellaneous Things* in 1926. It was a reflection on how we should hold in high esteem the plates, bowls, pots and pans that surround the lives of ordinary people – the folk crafts that have been handmade for centuries. In a similar way, I would like us to pay attention to the sounds, smells, colours, shapes and textures of everyday life.

Soetsu Yanagi's perfectly crafted sentence touches on something that is now well researched in the realm of creativity: the concept of 'flow'. This is when your mind drifts slightly, leaving your unconscious self alone to do wonderful things. Because our minds tend to wander more in the latter part of the working day, this seems the perfect time for a creative get-together or to get yourself lost in a creative stupor.

The power of self-distraction has long been used by creative thinkers. Einstein and Sherlock Holmes played the violin while they struggled with a mathematical problem or a devilish case, fixing part of their mind on one thing, which might allow another part to happen upon a moment of inspiration. What scientists call 'constructive distraction' can be intentionally induced, with the right level of sensory stimulus, and here's how you do it…

AN EVOCATIVE SOUNDSCAPE

In every area of scientific study, there are superstars within that field. John Bargh and Joshua Ackerman are the masters of touch. Professors Barry Smith and Charles Spence are the doyens of sensory taste. And Ravi Mehta and Juliet Zhu are the go-to team for creativity – you'll hear their names a lot in this section.

In order to research the effects of sound on creativity, Mehta and Zhu conducted a series of studies where people performed creative challenges in different conditions: with the background noise of a café, busy traffic, construction noise, and so on. The results show that a constantly changing background noise, with a steady volume and no sudden outbursts, unequivocally enhances creativity. But it must be constant, familiar and not repetitive, in order to maintain that perfect balance of distraction and focus.

But rather than settle for the background noises we

discussed earlier – the hubbub of a café or the murmur of voices – this is a chance to be creative. Use sounds that are evocative of what you're working on, to encourage associated thoughts to bubble to the top of your mind. If you're writing a script for a film that is set in New York, listen to a New York cityscape. If you're trying to come up with new investment ideas, maybe listen to a recording of a stock market trading floor. Design a beachfront hotel to the sound of crashing waves.

Otherwise, as with 'experience aromas' that you can use to help pitch an idea to a prospective client, you might think laterally about an emotion that encapsulates what you are doing. If your ideas need to be passionate and competitive, how about the sound of a football match? Try to think about what might help divert you enough to be creative, while also setting a beneficial scene. With the advent of all types of sound-based websites, it's possible to conjure up pretty much any atmosphere – and as ever, I've put a few on the *Sense* website.

There is a lot of evidence about optimal volume, too. Creativity is greatly reduced when background noise goes over a level of seventy-five decibels: which is quite loud – about the volume of a vacuum cleaner. Another study by Mehta and Zhu, this time accompanied by Amar Cheema, tested people's creative thinking with background noise at different volumes. Participants were asked to take a 'remote associates test', in which you are given three words and have to find a fourth that connects them – for instance: aid /

rubber / wagon. Answer: band. People's scores were the highest when the background volume was around sixty-five decibels, the level of noise in a busy restaurant. Try and judge if the noise in your surroundings are at a comfortable level – you might find it useful to download an app that measures the loudness of the noise in a room on your phone.

THE SMELL OF PLAY-DOH

Do you remember the smell of Play-Doh? Smelling it will make you more creative and better at problem-solving. In 2015 Nahid Ibrahim investigated the beneficial effects of what he calls 'mental time travelling' – the idea that smells can bring you back to a time of playful activities in childhood, and that these sensory memories will affect your performance. This research study asked people to perform a task called 'Duncker's candle problem': the challenge is to work out how to stick a lit candle to a wall without it dripping on the floor, using only a box of matches and a box of drawing pins. Participants had to solve the problem in rooms with different smells: one had a nice citrus smell and one had the smell of Play-Doh, while a control group were in a room with no scent. Performance was better when either aroma was present, but it was best in the room with the Play-Doh smell.

This idea of 'mental time travel' both recalls an activity – with Play-Doh it's creativity and play – and puts you in the beneficial state of constructive distraction, because of its distant familiarity. An important point when using aromas for this kind of application is that they have to be recognisable, so they aren't too distracting. If you lit a candle scented with vanilla, tonka bean, vetiver, rose blossom and musk, the smell may be pleasant but its various layers would occupy too much of your mental energy, which would have a negative effect on your creativity and focus.

You can actually buy a bottled scent of Play-Doh – it was made by a company called The Library of Fragrance for the brand's ninetieth anniversary. Otherwise you could do what I do when we have creative meetings and bring along some Play-Doh to put on the table. I go for blue...

BLUE

People are most creative in the presence of the colour blue – it is the ultimate 'cool' colour and has a physiologically calming effect on us. Mehta and Zhu have shown time and again that it is better to be calmer when you want to get creative ideas flowing.

In another one of their studies, participants were given a range of red or blue shapes and asked to put them together to create ideas for a child's toy. Independent evaluators, who looked at the ideas in black and white, judged the blue ideas to be more original. The red ones were seen as being more practical, which again confirms the colour as best for detailed, practical tasks. In the same study they also showed that people displayed more 'approach-motivated behaviour' – behaving more adventurously and being open to new ideas – around the colour blue.

Try to bring in blue whenever you are working on something creative: your brainstorming notepad should be blue, and keep a tub of blue Play-Doh on your desk. If you are in control of your office environment, paint the walls of breakout spaces a cool, calming blue, or get a blue table-top in a creativity-focused meeting room.

LOW LIGHTING

There has been lots of research to point us in the right direction for the best type of lighting for creative thought. Who did the research? Mehta and Zhu, of course, this time with Chen Wang and Jennifer Argo. They discovered that if you place people in rooms with a variety of lighting situations and ask them to perform creative tasks, there will be a profound difference. In dim lighting, people show less inhibition and more freedom when it comes to how they think. However, although they knock out a stream of new ideas, one study showed that the chances are that they will be less appropriate.

If you have the ability to control the lights in your office or home, consider setting them to change over time – there's evidence to suggest that the slow movement of light can help creative thinking. A gradual shift in tone or brightness every eight to sixteen seconds, like slow-changing Christmas lights, will create enough subtle background movement in your periphery to help a state of constructive distraction.

DON'T TIDY – A MESSY WORKSPACE IS GOOD

This element of the sensory prescription is an interesting one for people like me, who can't work if the area around them is messy. I can't get started until I've arranged the various scraps of paper, pens and miscellaneous items on my desk in some kind of orderly fashion – I say it's down to a mild case of OCD, but it's more likely down to my penchant for procrastination. However, in terms of stimulating creativity, this is evidentially the wrong approach.

One study placed participants in two rooms that were identical, other than the orderliness of items on a desk. The first had a few neatly stacked piles of files and papers, but in the other, the same files and papers were strewn around the desk. To test their creative thinking, the participants were told that a ping pong ball manufacturer wanted to come up with new uses for their product, and asked them to list ten new ideas. This strange conundrum was conceived by Kathleen Vohs, Joseph Redden and Ryan Rahinel from the University of Minnesota and is a variation of what's called an 'alternative uses task', developed by the American psychologist J. P. Guilford to measure creative thinking in 1967 (though originally with a brick rather than ping pong balls).

The results of the study showed that people in the disorderly environment produced more unconventional and 'creative' solutions, as well as a greater number of ideas. Cognitive performance was shown to be more conventional in the tidy environment, while our thought processes are less conventional when the space is messier. It's quite common for artists, writers, scientists and other innovative thinkers to have chaotic workspaces – from Mark Twain to Steve Jobs, many of the greatest minds are famous for keeping their working environments cluttered. In my case, I try to leave my workspace a little less structured than my mildly obsessive–compulsive tendencies would have it – I perform my usual procrastination ritual before I begin but let natural entropy take over as I work, helping my thoughts drift towards the obscure.

OPEN SPACES

As I covered in my introduction to the working day, the ceiling height of a room affects how we think. High ceilings make us feel freer and more open, and we consequently think differently. Juliet Zhu is behind this fascinating area of research. In one experiment, she sat people in rooms with either eight- or ten-feet-high ceilings and asked them to solve a series of anagrams that were made of words relating either to freedom – 'liberated' and 'unlimited' – or confinement – 'restrained' and 'restricted'. The idea is that whether you're feeling free or restricted, the appropriate words will be at the front of your mind. The results confirmed the hypothesis; people's response time with the freedom-related words was faster in the high-ceilinged room. Further experiments in the same study looked at the different ways people remember information and showed that the high-ceilinged room was better for more abstract thinking and connecting ideas in a less obvious way. The bigger your box, the more 'outside' it you think.

OTHER THINGS – PLAY-DOH, A PENCIL AND AN ARTIST'S SMOCK?

If you really want to go for it in a creative session with your colleagues, or are sufficiently secure in your own identity to dress up a bit, this is the perfect time to employ the powers of enclothed cognition and material priming. So many items have artistic connotations, and it is easy to put on an outfit or pop something on the table to trigger creative thoughts. A tub of blue Play-Doh is perfect, as it's instantly recognisable, makes people happy and also brings in the aroma and colour. Use a pencil for writing with rather than a boring ballpoint pen. You could even use a paintbrush, although it might not be particularly practical.

If you don't want to go 'full-on artist' with a beret and smock, wear something that makes you feel loose and free, and nonchalantly throw a wrap or scarf around your shoulders like arty types do. As we covered when we discussed getting dressed, wearing the same item or trinket whenever you do your creative work will build up an association, or you might wear something that reminds you of a time or person that you associate with creativity.

A SENSORY PRESCRIPTION FOR CREATIVITY AND CREATIVE THINKING

- **Sound** – Evocative soundscapes. Something that sets the scene, but is constant, familiar and not repetitive. No louder than sixty-five decibels, and not much quieter.
- **Aroma** – Play-Doh. You can get a bottled version of the scent, but otherwise keep a tub handy and pop it on the table before you begin.
- **Colour** – Blue. Have a blue work pad, and blue walls or a blue table if you can.
- **Lighting** – Low-level, to get you relaxed and help shed your inhibitions. If you can control them, a slow pulse in the lights might help.
- **Environment**: Messy, if you can handle it, with high ceilings.
- **Other Things** – The aforementioned tub of blue Play-Doh, unrestrictive clothing and accessories that will prime the right feelings.

Late Afternoon – Speeding Up Time

As the end of the day nears, the minutes might begin to drag. But no matter how much we know that clock-watching only makes it worse, it can't be helped. Especially as we're now surrounded by so many clocks – on your computer desktop, phone, wall and maybe on your wrist.

By now the dopamine should be kicking in a bit, as

expectation grows for the reward you planned earlier. There's nothing you can do to speed up time, but there is something you can do to speed up how you *perceive* it passing. First, remove all the clocks from your sight, and then set up this sensory prescription to make the seconds fly by.

SLOW MUSIC

Of all the senses, it's our hearing that can most affect how time passes; it seems counter-intuitive, but slow music in a minor key makes time pass more quickly. This is a proven effect that I once used to create a playlist of hold music for a bank's customer service phone line. With waiting times mounting, the number of complaints were greatly reduced by making customers listen to a compilation of Balearic chillout music as they sat hoping to be put through to a human. A ten-minute wait suddenly felt like five.

This effect is all due to arousal. Fast music speeds up the heart rate and makes you more alert, so you notice the passing of time more acutely. Slow music, on the other hand, is calming, slowing your heart rate and breathing. And because you're affected by the music's tempo, you perceive time to be moving slower, which means 'actual time' is moving more quickly than you think.

Similarly, music that is in a minor key is less arousing than happy music in a major key. In one study at Northwestern University, researchers had a piece of music written in both a major and a minor key, with both versions exactly the same in all other ways. They then arranged for 150 people to listen to a version of the track and estimate how long they thought it was. Even over a short period of time – the piece was two and a half minutes long – people's estimation of the time that had passed when the track was in a minor key was on average about forty seconds less than when it was major.

So for time to pass more quickly, listen to slow music in a minor key. You don't have to go for tear-jerking ballads or ambient chillout, but a playlist of laid-back and wistful tunes will see the last bit of the working day disappear before you know it.

A PLEASANT SMELL

Whatever the smell is, as long as there is one, and you like it, time will pass by more quickly; the last hour of the working day is definitely a good time to top up your perfume, light a scented candle, spritz something into the air or consume something fragrant. One study into the behaviours of shoppers in California involved observing 298 students, who were asked to enter and browse the aisles of a mock-up supermarket while the researchers filled the air with different scents. As well as measuring the amount of products the participants touched, the researchers also measured the time that each person spent looking around, before asking them afterwards how long they thought they'd been. As well as liking the store and the products more when there was a scent in the air, on average they thought they'd spent seventy-five seconds less in the shop when there was an aroma.

Interestingly, no one noticed the smell, which shows again how little we tend to focus on our senses and the effect they have on us. Even when you don't know it's there, having a nice smell in the air has a positive effect on the passing of time.

The stress of having to wait is also alleviated by a nice smell. One survey was conducted in one of the slowest-moving places on earth, a Department of Motor Vehicles waiting room – where poor souls wait for hours to get their driving licence or car registration. Even in this excruciating environment, a gentle waft of lavender aroma made the wait pass more easily, and, unbelievable as it is, people left satisfied with the level of customer service.

As the music you'll be listening to is slow and reflective, you'll want the scent to match it. I'd go with lavender, as it's a 'slow' scent, cross-modally speaking, and it goes with the calming colour that follows. But you need to like it, so choose what you think will make for a pleasant environment, ensuring that you match the other elements of the sensory prescription for a happy state of congruence.

CALMING BLUE

The emerging theme here is that the calmer you are and the nicer your environment is, the quicker time will pass. As we discovered earlier, cool blue is a physiologically calming colour. One study has not only corroborated this, but also provided a valuable tip for web designers. When forty-nine people were sat in front of a computer set up to mimic images loading on a website, they thought the time passed faster when the webpage had a blue background than when it was red or yellow. The people in the study also said that they felt more relaxed when the screen was blue.

The sensory prescription here is short and sweet, but perfectly formed. Music, scent and colour are the sensorial elements that speed up our perception of time, and brought together they form a simple trio that's easy to pull together when you need to. It's nice to know that when the hours are beginning to stretch on, popping on some melancholic music, spritzing a nice scent in the air and getting your blue notepad out will bring on the end of the working day more quickly and in a more relaxing state.

A SENSORY PRESCRIPTION TO SPEED UP TIME

- **Music** – Slow, down-tempo, wistful and melancholic.
- **Scent** – A nice, pleasant smell, but choose something soft and calming that goes with the music and the colour – lavender, jasmine or sage.
- **Colour** – Blue, or any other calming, cool shade, from green to turquoise or even soft pink.

Before you know it, the working day is done and it's time to go home. There are a few things you need to get from the supermarket on the way; in Chapter 7, I'll reveal some of the ploys I use to guide you around the store and communicate the qualities of different products. But before that, a sensorial sidestep into the world of touch.

CHAPTER 6

Touch

Touch is a sensation that we can't turn off. You can close your eyes, muffle your ears and hold your nose, but you are always touching something. Our skin is one giant organ that is dedicated to picking up the smallest sensations of temperature, texture, shape and weight; from the slightest breeze to whacking your thumb with a hammer, the range of sensation we can pick up is mind-blowing.

When we touch or are touched, we sense it in two ways. There is what is called 'discriminative touch', which tells us accurately where it happened, how gentle or forceful the touch was, what the texture was like and the direction of movement. Then there is 'affective touch', which comes from sensors in the skin called C-tactile fibres. Affective touch is less concerned with the specifics of the sensation but tells you if the touch is nice, like in a warm hug or a gentle stroke. This isn't two pieces of information coming from the same place and being interpreted differently; it's two completely different sets of receptors, one for factual sensing and the other for emotional feeling. It means that discriminative touch is always interpreted in the same way, while affective touch can be interpreted differently, depending on other factors – it's emotional, and emotions change with context or get coloured by other sensory stimuli.

For instance, the phrase 'hurt so good' can sometimes be true. Your muscles aching and your lungs burning might feel awful when you've just had to sprint to catch a train, but the same sensation after an intense workout in the gym buoys you up with a sense of achievement and you leave feeling better for it. A gentle caress can be repellent if it is uninvited. Imagine having an argument with your partner and them trying to hold you or offer a reassuring stroke; the contact might feel unwanted and manipulative. The discriminative touch is identical, but the feeling is entirely different.

The author David Linden, who wrote a whole book about touch, talks about a woman who lost her sense of touch because of a rare disorder called primary sensory neuropathy. She was unable to distinguish between textures, but could feel if a stroke on her arm was caring or not. She wouldn't be sure of where exactly she had been stroked, but would know it was pleasant – her sense of discriminative touch was impaired, but she could still feel affective touch.

Because our emotions are so influenced by the sensory information we receive, we can assume that our other senses interfere with how we interpret touch. For instance, it has been shown that a pleasant smell can make a material feel more pleasant, and that when it is imbued with an unpleasant smell, the same material feels less pleasurable. An early investigation into the cross-sensory aspects of touch was conducted by a psychologist called Donald Laird in 1932. He presented women with four identical packs of silk stockings and asked them to open them and evaluate the feel and quality. One pair was left smelling au naturel, while the other three were scented – one of which with the aroma 'narcissus', a deep green, floral, rich scent. The ladies preferred the stockings with the added fragrances, and the Narcissus-scented ones the most, but when they were asked why, they talked about their superior feel, sheen or weave. None of them mentioned the difference in aroma, despite the fact that they were otherwise exactly the same.

Our sense of touch can also be manipulated by what we hear; the sounds that materials make when we touch them greatly affect what they feel like to us. In one study, participants were asked to stroke different grades of sandpaper, while the researchers changed what they could hear. When the sound was dulled, essentially making it sound softer, the textures felt smoother; when the sound was turned up, the sandpaper felt rougher.

There is also a phenomenon called the 'parchment-skin illusion', discovered by two scientists from the Helsinki University of Technology in 1998, which shows that the sound we hear can even change the way our own skin feels. Participants were asked to rub their hands together in front of a microphone, with the sound being fed back to headphones that they were wearing, in real time. If the researchers made the sound thinner and high-pitched, the participants said their skin felt dry and coarse; if the sound was dulled, they said it felt soft and smooth. It's amazing that sound can override what you're feeling with your own skin – you'd have thought that your sense of touch would be pretty decisive in that situation.

We are even able to add a sense of touch when there is no actual touching involved, by using sound to trigger the sensation. I conducted a study with a group of digital interactive designers and the team at the Crossmodal Research Laboratory at Oxford. The designers had created an augmented reality experience that acted like a kind of digital mirror; standing in front of a large TV screen, you could see yourself wearing different jackets that you could switch between with the wave of your hand.

When it comes to clothes, we get so much information about them through touch, yet in the world of online shopping we are expected to evaluate them without being able to feel them. We regularly receive something through the post, only to discover that it feels cheap, that the material is uncomfortable or that it doesn't sit right – qualities that you would know instinctively with the simplest touch. In our study, we tried to counteract this.

We took two items of clothing that sounded vastly different – a fleece and a waterproof jacket – and recorded every noise they make when you move about while wearing them. The sounds were then mapped onto the application, so that you could stand in front of the screen and stroke the jackets, hearing the sound of the material through a pair of headphones. At the lab in Oxford, we then arranged for people to try it out with or without the sound. When we asked them afterwards whether they liked the items and how much they'd pay for them, the results showed that when the sound was present they liked the jackets a lot more and put their value at around 35 per cent higher. Being able to hear the materials, the participants could judge their quality; it made the experience more emotionally engaging and gave them more of an attachment to the product, which translates into value. This helps to show that our experience of a single sense that seems isolated is actually a combination of lots of other senses, all of which assist our perception.

The opportunity for the application of this kind of technology in online shopping is huge. If you could run your mouse over an image and hear the material, you would get a sense of the texture almost as clearly as holding it in your hands.

Removing the ability to touch something makes it virtually impossible to feel any emotional attachment to it. In an experiment that got people to perform day-to-day activities such as vacuuming, cleaning and eating while wearing thick gloves, the subjects said they felt emotionally detached from every experience – more so than when they got people to do similar activities when blindfolded. Not being able to feel blocked them off from the experiences more than not being able to see. Of course, the level of importance people place on touch varies from person to person; to quantify this difference, researchers came up with what is known as the 'Need for Touch' scale (NFT). People who are high in NFT will feel more alienated from items they don't get to feel, so will be less likely to make purchases online. To establish someone's NFT score, marketing professors Joann Peck and Terry Childers devised a twelve-point questionnaire, in which respondents log their feelings on a scale between -3 and +3 on the basis of how strongly they agree with each statement. Here are a couple of examples from the test:

- When walking around stores, I can't help touching all kinds of products.
- Touching products can be fun.
- I feel more comfortable purchasing a product after I've physically examined it.

People in my line of work can use the NFT scale to assess a brand or a product's demographic and determine whether

A prescription for Eating Healthily

Surround yourself with things that feel fresh, pure and natural, and you'll behave accordingly

Daylight and bright light

The smell of fresh herbs

Lower volume means healthier choices

Music with high-pitch bells adds sweetness without sugar

You'll eat less food with a red plate

Don't carry a bag when you shop for food

Smelling something indulgent for 2 minutes can satisfy and dispel your cravings

A prescription for Exercise

You're more likely to win a sport if you wear red

Listen to music you like

Choose bright clothing with angular geometric patterns

Work out with others to up your game

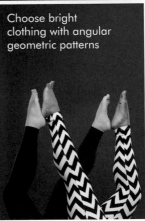

Exercising in nature enhances the benefits. But even a view or an image helps

Sharp shapes feel more active

Peppermint cools and invigorates

A prescription for Better Productivity

We're better at cognitive tasks in a red room

Bright blue-white light improves productivity

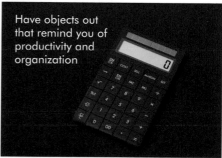
Have objects out that remind you of productivity and organization

The smell or taste of cinnamon enhances problem-solving and accuracy

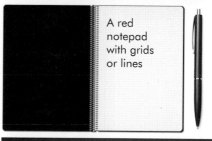
A red notepad with grids or lines

Sit upright and you feel more confident in your work

MIND YOUR POSTURE

Listen to upbeat music

A prescription for Pitching An Idea

Fill the room with plants

The clean scent of lime can make people more generous

Use a green notebook

Sit the decision-maker in a soft, comfy seat

Wear black and others see you as more confident

Spritz a scent that brings your idea to life

Hand over a solid folder and you'll come across as more competent

Make sure the room sounds soft and muted. Avoid echo and extraneous noise

A prescription for Collaboration

Hand out yellow notepads or folders

Round tables encourage openness

Serve soft food. Nothing crunchy

A playlist of gentle background music

Soft textures promote collaboration and generosity

Put some flowers out. The scent makes people more talkative

If all else fails, go clubbing to become a tribe among tribes

A prescription for Creativity

Blue notepad and pencil

Blue is calming and helps creativity

High ceilings lead to more moments of inspiration

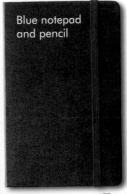

We're less inhibited in low lighting

The nostalgic smell of Play-Doh. And the sensory enjoyment of playing with it

Listen to evocative sounds that set the scene for what you're working on

Messy environments encourage creative thinking

A prescription for Sex

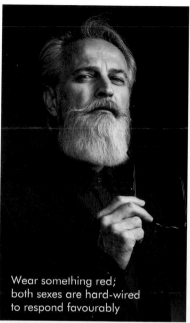

Wear something red; both sexes are hard-wired to respond favourably

Soft textures invite touch and awaken the senses

We're drawn to the scent of our partner's skin

Warm red-orange lighting

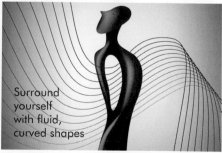

Surround yourself with fluid, curved shapes

Whispers and soft voices are intrinsically intimate

Warm, sweet, foodie aromas

A prescription for Better Sleep

Turn screens OFF! At least 2 hours before bed

Low, warm lighting

Bathe about 90 minutes before sleep if possible

Listen to relaxing music for 45 minutes before bed

Engage in a relaxing activity, like reading . . .

. . . or write down your plans for tomorrow

Chamomile and lavender

75

IN 2+ HR

17°C

16-19°C is the optimum temperature for a good night's rest

any tactile elements of the design need to be changed. For instance, when I was consulting on the packaging for a men's razor, we conducted a survey of the brand's target market and saw that 72 per cent of them had more trust in products that they could touch, and 85 per cent were more comfortable purchasing a product that they could touch. These results led to recommendations around exposing parts of the handle and departing from the generic plastic feel of the packaging, in order to enhance people's feelings towards the razors.

In the next chapter we will walk around a shop and explore some of the things that sensory marketeers can do to enhance the consumers' experience of products, through the design of their packaging and the broader retail environment. Touch will play a big part of it.

No matter how important touch is to you, the influence it exerts is profound, though it is mostly unconscious. We are not able to focus on every touch – it would be like listening to every single sound in our environment at the same time, turned up to equal volume. We have to filter most of it out, so touch drifts into the background and we don't realise how much it affects how we read a situation, feel about a place or person and evaluate whatever we come into contact with. As with all your senses, I hope this book will make you more aware of the presence of touch, pay attention to texture and touch the world around you a little bit more. But now it's time to go back to our day. Let's go shopping.

CHAPTER 7

Shopping

For a lot of people, the shop on the way home is a good place to pick up a few items, and maybe get that little treat that you planned earlier and see what else tickles your fancy.** But in this short trip to the supermarket, your senses are playing a huge part in how you behave and what you buy, and it's mostly beyond your control.

Before you start perusing the shelves, there are a couple of things you can do to influence your decision-making.

Making Healthier Choices

DON'T CARRY A HEAVY BAG
The decision to forget your diet and choose something indulgent is more likely at the end of the day, with

the mental strain of decision fatigue and ego-depletion in full swing.

Trudging into the supermarket with your bag slung over your shoulder is going to make things even harder. A research study in a university cafeteria examined the food choices people made when they were carrying light or heavy bags. When the bag was heavy, they chose unhealthier items than if their bag was light. The same effect was seen when they tried it with different weighted plates – people chose less healthy food when they were carrying a heavy plate. The researcher's explanation is that the burden of the weight reduces our 'regulatory resources'. Unable to regulate our will power and our pre-made decision to be healthy, we throw caution to the wind and go for the easier choice – something that looks filling and comforting. As you enter the supermarket, get a trolley and pop your bag in it – it will lessen your burden and help you stay in control of your own behaviour.

SMELL SOME INDULGENT SMELLS

If you're exposed to the smells of indulgent food for more than two minutes it gives you a feeling of sensory satisfaction, as if you've actually had the treat, and you will inevitably buy healthier food. A study by Dipayan Biswas and Courtney Szocs demonstrated this counter-intuitive effect by getting people to smell either cookie dough, pizza, apple or strawberries, before asking them to choose some food or drink. In one of the conditions of the experiment, subjects were exposed to a smell as they entered a supermarket and then left to shop, with their shopping basket analysed afterwards. It turned out that they bought more healthy items when they'd smelled cookie dough before they started shopping than when they'd sniffed strawberry. For the smell to have a positive effect, it has to be a prolonged exposure – the positive effect only kicks in after two minutes. Just getting a quick waft made things worse in the study, increasing cravings and the chance they would cave. So you might decide to carry something that smells sweet and enticing with you, or you could stand outside a fast food chain or bakery and take a good long sniff before you enter the supermarket.

Once you are inside, it's time to discover some of the devices that store designers use to entice you to purchase certain items over others. By focusing on each sense individually, let's look at all the clever placing of products on shelves, the colour and texture of the packaging and the background music and smells, the influence of which you may not be consciously aware of.

Sensory Influences in the Shopping Environment

SIGHT

As you enter the shop, the first thing that you see is rows of fresh fruit and vegetables, placed at the entrance to make the place look fresh. If you walked straight into the cleaning product section and were confronted with bleach, washing-up liquid and mops, the food beyond wouldn't seem so appealing. Seeing the colours and smelling some of the produce communicates freshness and vibrancy. A lot of supermarkets now use wooden crates with words like 'farm' or 'market' laser etched on them, to hint at authenticity and 'localness' – saying that, despite the scale of the megastore you're standing in, they are a down-to-earth grocer and connected to their roots.

When the shelves are stacked there is a design to their arrangement, and a power struggle between brands to get the optimal positions for their products, but it's not simply a case of getting seen. A study by Carlos Velasco, a key figure when it comes to this area of consumer neuroscience, discovered that the level on which different products are placed can impact on how much you want to buy them – because of the way we cross-modally relate taste to visual height.

The study determined that most people think of the concept of 'sweetness' as being high up and 'bitterness' as being low down. This matches up with what we know about links between music and taste – people relate sweet flavours with higher musical notes, while bitterness is mostly seen as quite low-pitched. Carlos and his team placed sweet and bitter products in different arrangements on some mock-up supermarket shelves. When the sweet products were higher up, participants found them more appealing than when they were low down. By placing the sweet items above the bitter ones – jam above Marmite in the breakfast spreads aisle, say – both products appear more appealing and customers will be more willing to buy them.

The packaging of the products is where the real action is. The colours, images and claims – everything there is designed to appeal to some kind of sensibility within you.

Since health is of prime importance in modern food trends, let's look at that. We instinctively link the colour green with health because it reminds us of nature. So if a product has green packaging, we presume it's healthier than an equivalent product with packaging that's a different colour. And if you're particularly health-conscious, you're more likely to make this assumption. And nor does it have to be the colour of the whole packet; a study by Jonathon Schuldt, a professor at Cornell University, asked ninety-eight students to imagine that they were hungry and standing at a supermarket checkout. They were presented with two snack bars, both of which were prominently labelled with the number of calories they contained. The number of calories was the same, but one label was red and one was green. The participants believed that the bar with the green calorie label was healthier, even though the number was the same. When presented with rational information in front of our eyes, we respond emotionally, based on a learned sensory association – green is natural, so this must be healthy.

Other colours have similar effects. We've already learned

that red is regarded as heavier than yellow. A study in Germany examined whether that cross-modal link translates into how we evaluate the calorific content of food and drink. A group of subjects were shown images of a made-up brand of fizzy drink, with cans that were either red or yellow. The people in the study expected the yellow cans to contain less sugar and fewer calories.

The pictures on food packaging can also greatly influence our idea of how healthy something is going to be. Let's imagine that a pack of biscuits has an image of corns of wheat on the front, and the one next to it has an illustration of the biscuit. Research shows that we will believe the one with the wheat to be more natural than the one with the drawing, and it will also taste purer. As I mentioned, when people are asked how much they care about healthy food, the ones who are more bothered about it are also more influenced by these visual cues.

Finally, if a written claim on the pack tells you about the product's health-giving benefits, such as '100 per cent whole wheat' or 'full of natural goodness', it has been shown that people believe it more when the claim is placed at the top – we relate health with lightness, and lightness with being higher up.

TOUCH

When you hold a packet of food, you fall prey to what is known as 'sensation transference', when the experience through one sense transfers to another quality, even though they might not be connected. If packaging material has a slightly rough texture, we expect the product to be healthy and more natural, the eco-friendly credentials that we attribute to recycled card being transferred onto our feelings about the food inside. For all you know, the ingredients might be full of chemicals and mass-produced in a factory owned by a huge conglomerate, but we are so influenced by our senses that rough-textured packaging makes us believe that whatever's inside is made by friendly people who care about the planet.

Whatever textures you experience, the sale is almost in the bag if you are touching the product at all. The longer we hold something, the more likely it is that we will buy it, because you feel emotionally attached to it – it's the endowment effect that we came across earlier. Marketeers, shops and brands are making ever more effort to get you to touch their products, in order to convince you to make a purchase. They might use a variety of textures in their packaging, so you're intrigued when you pick it up and consequently hold it for longer; anything that gives you a bit of tactile interest will increase the chance that you'll buy it.

Apart from feeling its texture, when we pick a product up we also feel its weight. The weight of packaging is a huge cue for attributes that we instinctually sense but might not register consciously. For instance, depending on the product, heaviness might make something seem more effective (if it's a cleaning product), more filling (if it's a nutritional food) or better quality. If the brand hasn't chosen to use heavier packaging in order to convey this (doing so would increase shipping costs), they might place images, text and darker colours at the bottom of a pack to make it feel heavier.

Midway through the supermarket are the chilled aisles, full of the really tempting and indulgent items. There's one element of touch that you can now control: your own temperature.

PUT YOUR COAT ON AROUND THE FRIDGES

There is one interesting piece of evidence about how the feeling of air on the skin can change our decision-making. According to research, we mentally 'thermoregulate'. Under normal circumstances this is a scientific way of saying that we put a coat on when we feel cold, but doing it mentally means that we make a cognitive decision to balance out our temperature in another way – through an instinctual choice. The research showed that when we're cold, we tend to buy more indulgent and rewarding products; when we're warm, we find it easier to make a sensible decision. In the study, people were either cooled down or warmed up, before being asked to choose between chocolate cake or fruit salad. The colder crew pounced on the cake, while the warmer bunch chose the fruit salad. Following on from this discovery, a survey measured the temperatures inside a range of high street stores; the more expensive shops, or those selling indulgent products like clothes, shoes, jewellery and upmarket cakes, were all colder.

So if you thermoregulate yourself with clothes when you go down the chilled aisles or are browsing in expensive boutiques, you'll avoid your natural reactions kicking in and making you splash out on something that might bring you a bit of comfort.

SMELL

It's easy to understand why food smells are used to entice us into a purchase; most of us have smelled the wafts of baking in the bread section of a supermarket, and know it is pumped in for effect. When in-store bakeries first started appearing in the mid-1970s, bread sales rose by 300 per cent. Coffee is a similarly beguiling aroma, as a recent study showed. A petrol station that sold freshly brewed coffee installed a TV screen by the pumps that played an advert for the coffee. Sales went up significantly, by around 80 per cent. When they added a machine that gave a burst of coffee aroma as the advert played, however, sales increased by 374 per cent.

In food and drink, the presence of scent is likely to be acknowledged, but beyond that world it can slip into the unconscious. Sensory marketeers like myself are then able to use them as a subtle backdrop to make you browse for longer, buy more and build a connection between a brand and your emotions. Scent envelopes you in an environment and accentuates qualities of the products on display. For instance, a Dutch lingerie brand called Hunkemöller created a scent using ingredients that cue up feelings of 'luxury' and 'softness', placing it in half of their outlets. All other things being equal, customers spent around 25 per cent longer browsing and spent around 30 per cent more per person when the aroma was in the air.

It's not simply a case of wafting whatever you fancy into a shop and reaping the rewards – you have to approach the process with scientific validity, or the effects can be detrimental. In 2005, a department store commissioned a survey to ascertain the preferences of their male and female customers. Two aromas were subsequently created: a sweet floral scent for the men and a vanilla one for the women. The aromas were pumped into the appropriate clothing departments, and sales doubled. However, when they switched the two scents around, sales fell dramatically. You can also easily overdo it. Some shops are famous for blasting overpowering aromas onto the street – if you've ever walked past a Lush soap store or a branch of Abercrombie & Fitch, you'll know what I'm talking about. It certainly helps with brand awareness, but it's also incredibly polarising – if you don't like it, you really don't like it. The best results always seem to be when the scent is at a low level and barely detectable.

If you get the intensity and the ingredients right, a 'brand aroma' can be a powerful asset that can be used effectively to recall emotional associations that you have with a particular shop or product. Say you walk into a clothes shop, excited to treat yourself to something nice. There's a gentle background waft of fragrance that you don't particularly notice; if done right, it should reflect the personality of the designer and the aspirations that you connect with their clothes. A gents' tailors might smell of leather, cedarwood and tobacco. You try on your suit or dress and decide to buy it. The cashier puts a little spritz of the fragrance onto the packing paper before wrapping your item and putting it in a high-quality tote bag, and you leave feeling sophisticated.

When you get home and open the bag, feeling excited at the thought of wearing the garment, you get another waft of the scent. From around this point, you have an emotional bond with that smell, which is directly attributed to that particular designer. From now on, whenever you smell it again, those feelings will come back. The company might send you something through the post, maybe a catalogue imbued with the smell, and a rush of emotional memories will flood back. Or if you walk past any other shop from the same designer, anywhere in the world, you'll get a waft. It's formidable and complex – so many layers of emotion, memories and associations are tied up with a single scent.

That's the power our sense of smell has over the other senses. It can trigger a memory, convey a physical quality, affect your behaviour and forge a new memory, all at the same time, mostly without you knowing.

TASTE

You don't do much tasting in the supermarket, unless you grab something from the deli to eat as you go around, or sample a soupçon of something at one of those promotional podiums. There's a lot they could do to make that little sample more delicious, but sadly it's usually just an uninterested staff member wearing an apron and plastic gloves handing out cheese on a plastic plate – not particularly appetising.

However, a lot is done in the packaging of food products to make you expect how tasty they will be. This continues to influence you until the moment that you eat it, improving your perception of the product's flavour and quality.

A deeper, richer colour, both instinctually and through learned associations, should mean a more intense flavour. If you made two drinks of cordial and one was darker than the other, you would know that it would have more flavour. We project this learned multisensorial association onto the packaging that food comes in. In one study, when people were asked to choose between coffee that was presented in yellow, blue and red jars, everyone expected the one in the blue jar to be weak, the yellow one to be mild and the coffee in the red jar to be richer and fuller of flavour.

The same ploy is used in the healthy products we looked at earlier. A barrier to people buying 'light' versions of products – from low-calorie foods to alcohol-free beer – is that they think they'll taste weak in comparison to their full-fat, full-alcohol counterparts. However, if their packaging features rich, bold colours, a shopper will think the flavour is going to be full, despite the lack of sugar. And like serving your breakfast and coffee in a red bowl and mug, that intensity of colour will also enhance how you perceive the flavour, which will appear fuller and richer.

Intensity of taste is linked to intensity of colour and other sensorially learned associations. Going back to touch, more weight will enhance flavour intensity, both in terms of what we expect it to be and also how it actually tastes. Putting the image of the food and the description of its flavour at the bottom of the pack adds up to something that appears to be fuller of flavour, while putting it at the top makes it seem lighter and healthy. Liquids flowing and splashing on packaging make drinks taste fresher, which is why milk and dairy products often have an image of the drink being poured into a glass on the bottom of the pack. Before we taste anything, we are being primed to expect the flavour; when done in line with what's inside, it will be tastier and more enjoyable, and we'll also happily pay more for the pleasure.

SOUND

The effect of background music in supermarkets has been known for a long time. When the music is slower, people move through the aisles more slowly, consider more items and buy more things. When the effect was tested in one supermarket, changing the tempo of the background music from 94bpm to 72bpm resulted in people walking 15 per cent slower, and sales increased by around 40 per cent.

There have been some interesting studies into the effects of different types of music on our shopping behaviour. For one week, a wine shop in Texas exclusively played classical music, and then they played chart music for another week. When the classical music was on, the average spend per customer went up by 40 per cent – because of the emotions and associations we have with classical music, it makes us feel and act more classily. In the wine shop, that emotional shift was reflected in customers' purchase decisions.

Back in the supermarket, another study looked at the choices people made when music from different countries was playing. For a week or so, a wine aisle in a branch of Tesco played stereotypically French music, and the next week they played German oompah music. Let's say that usually people buy four times more French wine than German, a ratio of four to one; when the French music was playing the ratio went up, say to eight to one. However, when the German music was playing, the sales flipped and German wine outsold French by around two to one. The shoppers were led in their choices by the not-so-subtle suggestions of the music that was playing. What's most interesting is that when people were asked if they'd heard the music as they were leaving the shop, bottle of Spätburgunder in hand, only 2 per cent of people acknowledged that it had affected their choice. The other 98 per cent not only claimed not to have noticed; they vehemently denied that it had had anything to do with their choice. 'I'm having Sauerbraten for dinner,' they would say. 'This is what I came here to get.' But the figures show that this can't be true.

CREATE YOUR OWN SENSORY JOURNEY

If you want to remove yourself from such atmospheric persuasion, you could always use the science to your advantage and immerse yourself in your own sensory world. Knowing that music and aromas sway our decisions and enhance our experience of products, you might select a playlist and an aroma, before guiding yourself around the aisles intentionally. Say you've planned to cook a curry tonight; if you put your headphones on with a Bollywood soundtrack and spray a spicy scent on yourself, perhaps with notes of cardamom, coriander or cumin, then excitement will build, emotions will rise to the surface and you will select all the ingredients with mouth-watering, tastebud-tantalising expectation. If you want to be more personal, then you could use something based on your own memories that you know will guide you around the shelves finding what you want, making the journey more of an emotional experience.

If you have been open and exposed to the environment of the supermarket, then by the time you get to the check-out, bottle of Australian Pinot Noir in hand because they were playing Kylie in the wine aisle, you might be feeling a little duped by the manipulation. However, I would argue that it's not a bad thing, when it's done well and with good intentions. It's an effective way of shortcutting information, enhancing our enjoyment of the products and the places where we shop.

For packaging, the sensory information and the experience have to match – as the old saying goes, 'you can't polish a turd'. If synthetic, cheap and sugary food is put in a natural-textured pack with images of fresh ingredients on the front, you may purchase it once, but you'll be disappointed and won't buy it again. If, however, the design and texture communicate the genuine properties of the product, then you've got what you paid for and it will taste even better because of what you've been 'primed' to expect.

When it comes to the wine, your choice may have been swayed by the music; but the research shows that if you listen to French music while drinking French wine, it will taste better. So having that musical memory in the back of your mind when you made the purchase will also contribute to making it taste better when you get round to opening it.

Beyond the products, these sensorial additions to shopping can make the whole thing more enjoyable, immersive and tantalising – more of an actual 'experience' that makes it worth going into a shop rather than shopping online. With high street sales dwindling, stores are becoming more about selling an experience than the items on the shelves. Some places are beginning to dispense entirely with stock, choosing instead to allow access to their online catalogue so you can order what you want and have it delivered. The outlet itself is just a place to experience the brand – to get the richness and warmth of interaction that you can't deliver digitally.

As a consumer, and we are all consumers, it is important to be aware of what's going on, as marketeers get more sophisticated. We want to feel like their 'tricks' are being done *for* us rather than *to* us. As with every part of your life, tune your senses and don't take everything you're experiencing for granted.

CHAPTER 8

Smell

If you had to choose to lose one sense – your sight, hearing, or sense of smell – which do you think you'd go for? Which would have the greatest impact on your happiness and quality of life? To lose sight would surely be devastating. Imagine being condemned to a world of darkness, unable to see your children. No more watching films, viewing art or taking in an awe-inspiring view. Every simple task, from getting dressed to cooking a meal, would become an unimaginable feat. Losing your hearing seems almost as disastrous. Imagine no more music – never being able to hear your favourite tunes again. But also consider how it would feel to be cut off from the world around you, with your life on mute. Missing out on the hubbub of a café or a bustling market. The chatter of friends and family around a dinner table. The voices of your loved ones.

But what about not being able to smell anything? The tantalising aromas of food is the biggest issue to most people; imagine not being able to smell bacon, coffee or freshly baked bread. And the smells of the outdoors, from freshly cut grass to the moment after it rains in the summer and the ground releases that unmistakable aroma, known as petrichor. But would losing all that be as bad as losing your sight or your sense of hearing? In comparison it seems slightly innocuous compared to the impact that losing either of the other two would have on your life. To those of us who are fortunate enough to have all their faculties, a life without seeing or hearing is almost unimaginable, but a life without smell doesn't seem too bad.

However, the evidence shows that we'd be wrong to think this – smell is a deceptively important sense. A comprehensive review of research conducted on the subject, by a group at the University of South Carolina, shows that 76 per cent of people with anosmia – the total loss of smell – suffer from severe depression, anxiety, and feelings of detachment and vulnerability. This figure is way more than those who lose their hearing or sight. Firstly, losing your sense of smell also means losing your sense of taste, as the two are closely connected. Not being able to taste food would result not only in losing the pleasure of eating, but in the loss of appetite. Sufferers of anosmia consequently report not wanting to socialise over food, which leads to a huge loss of connection with other people, and of shared experiences. Additionally, aroma has been crucial to our evolution because we are constantly picking up airborne particles that relate to family, friends, threats, attraction and other people's physical or emotional state.

As we'll talk about in the chapter devoted to sex, scent is the most powerful sense when it comes to sexual attraction. Without a sense of smell, sexual appetite and any sense of intimacy disappears. People with anosmia also report being anxious about not being able to detect danger because they can't notice the presence of smoke or gas in the air or tell if food is off. Sufferers report social anxiety from not being able to smell themselves and notice if they have body odour; everything stacks up to a state of alienation, detachment and anxiety.

The fact that taking away something that might seem to be almost superfluous to our existence – a 'nice to have' – impacts our lives so profoundly that for some it's not worth carrying on shows how multisensory we really are.

Our sense of smell is the oldest sense in terms of our evolutionary development, and also our most primitive. The part of our brain that processes aroma – the olfactory bulb – gave rise to the creation of the limbic system, the network of neural structures that is responsible for the processing of emotions; the two are indelibly connected. The olfactory bulb is three synapses away from the area of the limbic system that processes memories, whereas the visual cortex is thousands of synapses away. According to research carried out by the Rockefeller University, our short-term memory of aromas is on average seven times stronger than our memory of anything visual. In the long-term, scent memory is the most vivid and the most emotional. One of the earliest studies into what is termed 'autobiographical memory' – the ability to recall moments in your life through sensory stimulus – was written in 1935 by Donald Laird. He and his colleague H. B. Fitzgerald carried out a survey of aromas as 'revivers of memories and provokers of thoughts in 254 living men and women of eminence'. The subjects recalled memories of scents that were on average thirty-six years old with a clarity and intense emotional resonance; memories from almost four decades before were brought right back, just by smelling something.

This effect has come to be known as the 'Proust phenomenon', after the French author's description of it in *Remembrance of Things Past*. The oft-cited passage in which the narrator recalls the moment the memories of his childhood returned to him as he ate a madeleine soaked in tea includes the line, 'The smell and taste of things remain poised a long time, like souls, ready to remind us.'

When the smells and tastes have negative memories, the emotions tend to be more powerful. Think about an alcoholic beverage that you overindulged in at some point during your youth. For lots of people it's tequila; for me and many others who grew up in 1980s London, it's Thunderbird wine. One whiff and the feeling of sickness comes back to me in an instant. There is actually a reason why a smell can evoke disgust more powerfully than anything else; it's that evolutionary link back to the sense's original purpose. It's important for us to remember what bad smells are because it allows us to sense danger in the air or to tell if food is rotten – more useful for our ancient ancestors in life-or-death situations than being reminded of your aunt's tea parties or the whimsical joys of youth.

When we smell something bad, there's an interesting effect on our moral judgement; it's been proven that we tend to lean towards more extreme moral standpoints when a scent makes us feel disgusted. A study at Stanford University took 120 students and asked them to make a series of moral judgements, while a can of 'fart spray' left a lingering and unpleasant smell in the air. The participants had to indicate their level of disgust in response to various scenarios; one was about the legalisation of marriage between first cousins and another was whether a person was right to drive a short distance to work instead of walking. The stronger the smell, the more disgusted they were by all the scenarios, but only 3 per cent of them acknowledged that the smell had influenced their decisions.

I used this research to devise a campaign for World Animal Protection, a charity supporting the rights of farm animals. We created flyers that had photographs of different countries' favourite fast food – the ones in the USA had a bucket of fried chicken, while the UK version featured a bacon sandwich. Also on the front of the flyer was a peel-back tab that released a scent when it was lifted. Members of the public were handed a flyer and prompted to take a smell, but peeling the tab released a waft of a rather unpleasant smell we had created. Then, on opening the flyer, they would see a photograph of an unhappy factory-farmed chicken or pig; in their state of disgust due to the smell, they would respond in a more morally judgemental way. At this point they were asked to sign a petition to stop factory farming – the campaign was a success and we got more than 20,000 signatures.

The concept also played on the idea of context; sniffing an unexpected bad smell when you were looking at a bucket of fried chicken made it even worse. Another study showed that a single smell can be construed as either good or bad, depending on how it is framed. Rachel Herz and Julia von Clef from Brown University presented aromas to people, but gave them different verbal descriptions beforehand. When one of the scents was handed to subjects and presented as 'Parmesan cheese', it was met with moans of pleasure. Later on in the study, the same aroma was handed to the participants but described as 'sweaty socks'; this time the subjects instantly recoiled in horror.

We inevitably have a few scents that are personal to ourselves because of a specific moment in our lives when they were present. However, there are other scents that almost everyone will associate with the same emotions. For instance, if you have some sun cream squirrelled away in a bathroom cabinet, crack it open – especially if you're reading this in the depths of winter and need a boost. Take one whiff. Is your feeling positive or negative? Virtually everyone will say positive. Why? Because you tend to be happy when you use sun cream. After all, the scent signals the start of summer and thus positive memories of long days and going on holiday – and so smelling it brings back these memories.

I should add a caveat: if you currently have young children, your positive emotional associations with the smell of sun cream might have been replaced with stress and anger caused by desperately trying to slap it on them while they squirm and complain. But that should only be temporary – as soon as they have accepted that its application is a necessity, you should once again experience a rush of joy whenever you get a waft of it.

We should celebrate our sense of smell and use aroma throughout our lives. You can use it to lift your mood as well as to enhance more practical behaviours like being productive, making healthier choices or feeling more confident, as you'll learn elsewhere in this book. You can even use it for a bit of sensory time travel – Andy Warhol used to change the fragrance he wore every few months, so that if he wanted to return to a certain time, he could open a bottle of whatever he had worn then and be taken straight there.

The power of scent is much more pronounced when it has personal meaning, so try to collect more smell memories. When you travel, or when something wafts your way during an important experience, write down what it was for later reference. It's a lovely thing to be able to time travel through your memories, and it's always nice to know that if you need a lift or want to feel excited, sexy, youthful or angry even, you've got a personal trigger that's readily accessible.

CHAPTER 9

Home

When the working day is over, we have a desperate need to switch our mindset. After a long day concentrating on being productive, confident, collaborative and creative, we need to stop. The fact that many of us are not able to do so is an endemic problem.

When we return home for the day, each of us walks into a unique situation. Every home is different. You might have a bustling house of children, and perhaps your husband, wife, partner or nanny is there already, coping with the mayhem. Or perhaps it's all up to you. You may live in a shared house with a bunch of friends, or you might be walking into a quiet but warm home that you share with an animal companion. Whatever your situation, we need to make the transition from work life to home life clear and the evening ahead the best it can be. Taking a multisensory approach can mean creating a more emotionally supportive space or getting the best out of whatever you choose to do. This is precious time when you can be yourself and indulge in things that make you happy, so you need to try and make it as perfect as you can.

The Coming-Home Ritual

One thing that most of us will have in common is the performance of some kind of ritual when we come in. Maybe you pause in the hallway to drop the keys in a bowl by the door, take off your shoes and coat and put them all in their place. You may go straight into the kitchen and switch on the kettle, or you might go up to your bedroom and change your outfit as soon as you walk through the door. Whatever it may be, most people have something that they repeatedly do whenever they come home from work. These rituals might evolve organically due to what you're always carrying and the layout of your home – you might put a bowl on the table by the door because otherwise you can never find your keys; the banister is directly ahead of you and it's a good place to hang your coat. Or they may be entirely intentional; doing something that signifies the feeling of 'home' is a way to shed the work day and start the evening. Popping the kettle on is a classic – the bubbling sound triggers feelings of warmth, comfort, friendliness and the emotions linked to our sense of 'home'.

HOME

The importance of rituals in our enjoyment of everyday life is significant. Performing seemingly arbitrary routines before we engage in an activity is a way of triggering memories and emotions – their repetitive nature creates a link to the feelings that surround what we are about to do. From an athlete arranging their water bottles in a line before a race to running your finger down the centre of a Kit Kat to break the foil before cracking the bars open, rituals are proven to improve performance and enjoyment.

The 'coming-home ritual' is no different; it's an important behavioural signifier that work is over and the evening has started. Regardless of whether your evening plans involve watching TV or going out dancing, there has to be a clear punctuation mark beforehand. The overall goal for this ritual is to calm the body and the mind, which doesn't mean that everything you do has to be meditative and dreamy. A nice gin and tonic after a day's work is calming, but it's also a bit of a pick-me-up, and the process of putting one together is a ritual in itself. As long as whatever you do brings you into the moment and slows down your pace – slowing down is the first step to stopping.

We have learned a lot of information during the day about how to focus, relax and create a mindful moment. Now is the time to bring those tips together with some other nuggets of scientific insight, to create the perfect coming-home ritual to kick off the evening.

BUY FRESH FLOWERS

We keep coming back to the benefits of plants and flowers – they lower anxiety, help us recover from illness and get people talking and collaborating. Having plants in your home will improve your mental and physical health, especially if you don't have views onto a garden or trees. One piece of research that backed this up was run by a group in Tokyo, who asked people to sit in front of a vase of roses for four minutes. Another group sat in an identical room with no flowers. Each person was then asked to complete a questionnaire, while they were hooked up to a monitor. The people who had been in the room with the roses had lower heart and breathing rates, and reported feeling more comfortable, relaxed and natural while they answered the questionnaire.

On top of the physiological and psychological benefits of having flowers in front of you, there is a lot of ritual and pleasant feeling bundled up with a nice bouquet. They symbolise care and thoughtfulness; even if you bought the flowers for yourself, they still feel like a treat. The process of unwrapping, pruning and arranging them is a slightly-distracting-but-not-too-demanding process that detaches your mind from the goings-on around you, calms the soul and might lead to a moment of inspiration. The Japanese art of *ikebana* takes this to a whole other level, expressing emotion and reflecting life for those who practise it. You don't have to go that far; but try to do a little more than just plonking them in a jar – it's not like you do this every day, so unwrap and arrange them as part of your ritual. On the days when you don't have a new bouquet to arrange, place the flowers somewhere near where you spend time. As soon as you're home, you'll be reaping the health-giving, relaxing and existential benefits of a nice arrangement.

TOUCH WOOD

The same Tokyo-based scientists behind the roses study mentioned above conducted another piece of research that led them to conclude that touching wood lowers stress levels, calms the nerves and slows the heart rate. In this study, eighteen female participants were asked to sit for one minute with their eyes closed, before placing their hands on a block of solid material for ninety seconds. Before they opened their eyes, a researcher covered the block with a cloth so the subjects couldn't see what it was. They were then asked a few questions and had their heart rate and brain wave activity measured. They did this a few times with different materials: oak, marble, tile and stainless steel. Physiologically, people were much more relaxed when they were touching the wood, with the stainless steel causing a spike in brain activity related to an increase in stress. Psychologically the participants said they felt a greater sense of comfort and relaxation, warmth and 'natural-ness' while touching the wood, while stainless steel made them feel the most emotionally cold.

Several other studies have showed that touching artificial materials like PVC, denim and, again, stainless steel increases blood pressure and induces feelings of stress. The main researcher behind these investigations, Yoshifumi Miyazaki, believes that the effect is due to what he calls the 'back-to-nature theory', similar to the 'biophilia' that we have already encountered. Miyazaki has written many books on the therapeutic benefits of getting out into a forest, and believes that we have an innate connection to nature because we've only spent 0.01 per cent of our species' evolutionary history in the modern built environment.

Miyazaki argues that we enter a relaxed state whenever we are exposed to anything that relates to the natural environment; bringing natural materials into our homes is part of maintaining this connection and experiencing the emotional and health-giving benefits of nature. If that means sitting at a wooden table, you can do that as part of your ritual when you get in from work. Or maybe you could serve a coming-home snack on a wooden chopping board, making a difference to your enjoyment of the food and giving you a natural connection where there otherwise may not be one.

PICTURES AND OTHER THINGS – 'SOCIAL SNACKING'

Photographs of friends and family, places visited, adventures had and memories made form an important part of our home decor, along with objects acquired throughout our lives. All these things provide tangible reminders of our connection to the past and to other people that help to define who we are. Social psychologists have referred to these artefacts as 'social snacks'.

Every time you walk past a picture or an object, you will get a little emotional lift – a rush of a memory and the feeling that you are not alone. They have a positive effect on our wellbeing, helping to fend off feelings of loneliness and giving us a sense of belonging. They also have the power to instantly imbue a space with warmth. Wherever you perform your coming-home ritual, they should be present and prominent. Whether you go to the hallway, kitchen or bedroom as soon as you come home, have something on the wall that you can mull over for a moment while you kick off your shoes or make yourself a drink. It will help to bring in the positive feelings of home and remind you who you are.

AN ACTUAL SNACK, OR AT LEAST A DRINK

Food and drink often signify a moment of calm. They can also act as a reward for having achieved a certain goal or accomplished a task, like struggling through the door with shopping bags and kids after a long day at work. It's a good idea to add an element of taste to your ritual that signals the start of the evening, and eating and drinking is all about ritual – short, repetitive processes that delay gratification, build expectation and snap you out of an overactive mindset. Opening a bottle of wine, for instance, has a strong ritual element. Finding the corkscrew. Slicing the foil around the top. Taking out the cork, before a sniff, a pour, a swirl, another sniff and a sip. It's a long process, with each action building expectation, calming the nerves and slowing you down. By the time you have a taste, you'll already feel a mental and physical benefit. Of course, it doesn't have to be alcoholic. Performing any kind of food-or-drink ritual diverts the mind to the point of constructive distraction where thoughts slow and inspiration might creep in.

When you then sit down to tuck into your treat, make sure you take the time to enjoy the taste – it's no good eating something while you walk around picking up washing. There needs to be a mindful moment of reflection, where you're concentrating on the taste and the texture, that takes you away from your buzzing and bustling mind.

CREATE YOUR OWN 'BRAND AROMA'

This final element of a coming-home ritual is potentially the most powerful sensory enhancement – involving your sense of smell. Aroma touches you as soon as you walk in, acting as an immediate sensory-emotional signifier that you're home. In the same way that scent can be used as a powerful brand asset by companies wanting to forge an emotional link with you, you can create a link between a scent and your fondness for being at home. Give your abode a sensory identity, something that will trigger a sense of safety, warmth and comfort as soon as you smell it. Leave a reed diffuser by the door, ready for when you get back, or position an atomiser in the room where you perform your coming-home ritual.

Alternatively, you might choose to add the lighting of a scented candle to the list of things you do when you get home, to help this step change in your day.

The scent itself is a matter of personal choice, and we'll come onto the broader subject of scents for your home shortly. If I were trying to identify a sensory identity for a brand, I would go through a tried-and-tested process. The first step of honing down your personality and deciding which aromas embody your character is a lengthy process involving several workshops and stacks of Post-it notes. But beyond that, we have to think about the aroma's function: what do you want the scent to do? At this point in time, the purpose is to welcome and warm the soul, calming and slowing the mind and body.

When it comes to calming aromas, we came across the compound D-limonene earlier. It's found in citrus fruits and in wood oils like cypress, pine and cedar, and brings on a physiological and emotional state of relaxation. Lavender is also proven to have calming properties, along with many other floral scents. Both wood and flowers have come into play already, so either would be a good addition in terms of sensory congruence. There are many other aromas that have been shown to induce similar sensations of calm, from the warm notes of vanilla to the brighter, zestier orange or rosemary. Choose what fits for you, but the key is to use it regularly and to be consistent. Have the same scent waiting for you by the door, and use it whenever you get home from work.

THE POWER OF YOUR SENSES

At this point, many other sensory elements can come into play. Putting music on can be hugely effective; if it calms you and helps you identify with being at home, do it. Having the heating set to the same temperature with a thermostat will add another level of sensorial consistency; over time, if you do the same things every day, you'll build a strong emotional trigger that helps to switch your mind from busy to calm and from work to home.

A SENSORY PRESCRIPTION FOR A COMING-HOME RITUAL

- **Flowers** – Fresh flowers are calming and give an emotional lift, and the process of arranging them provides moments of zen.
- **Material** – Wood. And generally natural materials. If you have a wooden table, sit at that. Or serve a snack on a wooden chopping board gastro-pub style.
- **Pictures** – Place pictures of loved ones and past adventures near where you perform your ritual. Social snacking helps remind you of who you are, makes you feel connected and gives another boost of emotion.
- **Taste** – Serving yourself a snack or a drink is a ritual in itself. It adds an extra sensory layer to the ritual and slows you down while you focus on enjoying it.
- **Aroma** – Create your own home 'brand aroma'. A reflection of your tastes and a sensory signifier that you've crossed the threshold and are home.

Once the effect of your coming-home ritual has taken hold, you can start to think about the evening ahead, applying a multisensory approach to the atmosphere of the house as a whole. I believe that being at home should be an emotional journey whichever room you're in, but you should make sure you're doing the right things in the right room.

The Emotions and Functions of Each Room

An important psychological factor for enjoying your home environment is the preservation of the sanctity of each space. Each room or area within a space has a purpose and a function, so we need to be respectful of that and not distort it. Bedrooms are for sleep and sex, not work and TV. Lounges are for relaxation, rest, social gatherings; maybe sex too, but not while you have people over. If it all gets confused and mixed up, you'll have no way of transitioning between different activities or emotional states. In the same way the coming-home ritual signifies a clear change over from work to home, you need to be able to move to a different space to mark the end of one thing and the start of another. If you've been working in the lounge, where will you go when you've finished? If you and your partner lie in the bedroom talking about bills and arrangements for the school holiday, how do you switch to sex or sleep? Get these things out of the way in the appropriate places and then switch rooms to switch your mindset and behaviour, using scent and other elements to help define the changeover.

A recent survey sought to establish the common emotional associations that we attribute to different rooms in the house. Researchers asked 200 participants to choose the words they felt summed up 'the most important emotions and perceptions' that they would want each of the rooms to evoke within themselves. Here are some of the results; see how much you agree with them:

HALLWAY

'Inviting' was almost unanimously agreed to be the first feeling you want when you walk into a home.

LIVING ROOM

'Relaxation', 'family', 'comfort', 'cosy' and 'togetherness' were the top words chosen, with a reasonably even split between them.

KITCHEN

The largest proportion of people selected the word 'organisation' for the kitchen, with 'productivity', 'family' and 'abundance' all close runners-up.

MASTER BEDROOM

'Romance' took the largest piece of the pie, with 'comfort', 'relaxation', 'love' and 'privacy' also feelings that people associated with the room.

BATHROOM

The most popular emotions linked to the bathroom were 'relaxation' and 'rejuvenation'.

These results would suggest that a kitchen is the best place for getting home chores and work done, as well as being a place for socialising and celebrating 'abundance'. The living room needs to feel soft, comforting and promote togetherness – it should not be a place for sorting out the home finances. Bathrooms need to feel fresh for 'rejuvenation', but also to be a place where you can relax. You may have a tendency to spend hours in the bedroom, playing with the kids or talking about boring stuff with your partner, but intimacy should be the main concern and anything else will detract from that. Furthermore, all the research says that you'll sleep better if you find somewhere more appropriate for most other activities, and leave the bedroom until later on in the evening.

We may not all agree with these room-specific emotions and functions, and we may like a bit more crossover. Also, many people don't have such separate rooms, so a lot has to happen in one space. It's worth trying to perform the exercise yourself – ask yourself what you want each room or area to embody, and then see what you can do to keep each one as 'pure' as you can. When you know what each room is for, you can then use the sensory environment to bring it to life.

Beyond a complete interior design overhaul, the easiest way to do this is through aroma. Scents can be introduced easily and changed depending on how you feel, what you're up to, the time of the day, or the season. But we should consider using a different type of scent – what I tend to call 'experiential' aromas rather than layered perfume blends or individual ingredients – fragrances that remind us of past experiences. All around the house I believe we should try to create a journey of nostalgia and discovery, using smells that stir your emotions and tell a story.

Scenting Your Home – An Emotional Journey of Discovery

When we were discussing how to be creative at work, I talked about the idea of emotional time travelling – using the power of aromas to evoke feelings from the past, like the scent of Play-Doh to improve our capacity for creative thinking. A study by the consumer psychology professor Ulrich Orth showed that when a scent triggers a nostalgic memory, it causes what is called an 'emotional-motivational response', a fleeting rush of positive feeling that stirs up the desire to discover new things. They tested a variety of smells on 281 people to determine which ones evoked the strongest feelings of nostalgia; from a list that included blackberry, cinnamon and citrus blossom, the smells of baked bread and freshly cut grass came top. They are both linked to real moments in life when our emotions are active, and aromas that remind us of past experiences stimulate the strongest emotions.

In my work we use such nostalgic and 'experiential' aromas all the time. People make an instant connection with these smells, which tell them a story about where they are, the objects in the room and the features and function of the space, encouraging them to feel certain feelings. We often begin by taking what's already there in a space, and accentuate its natural smell; at other times we use something that is more abstract but connected to the vibe of the room, in order to evoke an emotion or trigger a thought. For example, when we were designing a scent for the dealerships of a luxury car manufacturer, we selected ingredients that embodied everything customers associated with the company and dispersed them throughout the space. Around the cars you could smell English oak, which evoked craft and prestige. In the room where you selected the interior, a background note of leather emphasised the material samples on display. Around the payment desk, there was a smell of freshly cut grass, stimulating a state of adventurous sensation-seeking and bringing to mind the great outdoors, through which the customer would soon be driving – top down, toupee blowing in the wind. Every scent we used carried with it a feeling that enhanced the space and the products on display, making the walk around the dealership a journey of emotional discovery.

We should approach the scent of our homes in exactly the same way, using these 'experiential' and nostalgic aromas to make every moment more emotional and rewarding. Think back to when you've been on holiday and rented a lovely old cottage. Imagine walking into the rustic kitchen of a French country home and being hit by the smell of fresh bread. Step onto the porch and the scent of lavender and jasmine. Walk into the lounge and the smell of burnt wood from an open fireplace, rather incongruous with the time of year but so evocative and steeped in authenticity. We always walk around picturesque places in this way, attuned to our senses and relishing the richness of the experience, enjoying little moments of wonder. So why shouldn't we do the same thing at home? Having your senses tantalised every time you walk into a room is such an enjoyable experience.

Just like a sensorial version of social snacking, you can create an evocative atmosphere that tells your personal story and connects you to the warmth of people in your life and places that are important to you. This is a time to play around and have fun with different scents. Here are a few suggestions to get you started:

WOOD

Notes of cedar, English oak and sandalwood have a great effect on a room and also on your emotions. Warm and woody scents evoke notions of craft and authenticity, and increase perceptions of 'luxury' and 'expensiveness' when they are used in shops and hotel lobbies. They also have a calming quality that according to Yoshifumi Miyazaki is down to the 'back-to-nature theory' that causes touching wood to affect our physiology. Another Japanese study measured the effects of cedarwood oil and found that it lowered stress and anxiety. If a room contains a lot of wooden furniture or your lounge has wooden floors, a subtle woody scent would draw out the material's natural beauty. It is an intrinsically inviting scent, so would also work in a hallway.

FRESHLY CUT GRASS

Cut grass may seem like an odd scent to use inside a home, but it brightens up rooms so effectively – when used around light colours and soft, natural materials, it feels like a perfect fit. The scent brings a sense of open space to a room, while also increasing the 'back-to-nature' element of the sensory environment. And as Ulrich Orth's study into the link between scent and nostalgic memories showed, it also brings out sensation-seeking behaviour – great if you want people to feel more adventurous in the space, like in a living room, where family get-togethers are so important. In a research study I conducted as part of a project for the governing body of British Summer Fruits, we proved that the smell of freshly cut grass and the taste of strawberries were the two sensory stimulants that evoked the strongest feelings of happiness in the British public, especially when they were combined.

In a 2015 survey into the nation's favourite smells, freshly cut grass came in third, closely behind baked bread and sizzling bacon. It's an easy aroma to replicate – I use an essential oil called galbanum, which is one of the key compounds that's released when grass is cut. It's easy to get hold of, and because it's so evocative, lots of scent designers and brands make their own blends to use as home scents, perfumes or scented candles.

LINEN

The smell of newly laundered linen is hugely evocative – who doesn't love the sensation of climbing into a bed with freshly cleaned sheets? It also reminds us of the outdoors and fresh air, perhaps because we associate clean laundry with the sight of sheets blowing in the breeze on a washing line. On a work project, I used the scent of linen in some immersive sensory 'pods' that we designed for a hotel. The idea was that you sat inside them and looked up at a screen onto which a blue sky with little fluffy clouds rolling by was projected, accompanied by the sound of a gentle breeze and the fresh linen scent. The three elements worked perfectly together and the experience was calming, refreshing and revitalising.

Research conducted by a large detergent manufacturer showed that people thought a pile of white laundry scented with fresh linen was cleaner and whiter than either an identical unscented pile or one that was scented with citrus. The smell of linen is pretty easy to get hold of. Use it in the bedroom in the morning, or to make a living room feel soft, clean and fresh, like a glorious spring breeze has just swept through the room.

PETRICHOR

Petrichor is the name given to the smell in the summer after it rains. As the heat of the sun beats down, natural oils and bacteria rise to the surface of plants, earth, roads and pavements. When the rain falls, the oils are released into the air and that beautiful, heady aroma is released. It's so evocative because it only happens in the summer and under the right conditions and for many of us it is tied up with specific memories and very tangible emotions. But our connection to it may go further back than that. Australian anthropologists believe we have an evolutionary link to the smell, because it signalled the first rain of the summer and the prospect of crop growth that our ancestors relied on for survival. These days, it's simply a lovely, nostalgic scent.

Off-the-shelf versions of petrichor, created by imaginative perfume designers, can work anywhere, but the bathroom might be the most fitting place. With splashes of water on the floor and the sound of the shower, the smell of the summer's first rainfall completes the scene beautifully. If your goal is to make the room feel relaxed and rejuvenating, petrichor is the perfect scent.

HERBS AND SPICES

My work partner Jo and I once installed the smell of fresh herbs – sage, rosemary and bay – in the winter vegetable aisle of the food department in a much-loved British high street retailer – it conjured up feelings of cosy evenings at home, and the comforting waft of a hearty dinner bubbling away on the hob. The scent made the vegetables more appealing, and they were consequently bought in greater numbers. As soon as the season changed, we returned to the shop to swap the scent – spring had come and a new palette of ingredients needed to be introduced.

The smells of food are so evocative and pleasure inducing, and the use of herbs and other aromatic ingredients has the ability to conjure up times of the year, experiences and travels. Every foodie moment and place has its own flavour identity. Cloves remind us of Christmas, while rose water might transport you back to a holiday in Morocco. We all have our own taste memories, as well as tons of culturally shared ones. The smells of food draw people together and can be a conduit to help you tell a story of your life.

In your kitchen at home, the scent should reflect your journeys, the seasons and the food you want to eat. Maybe that would mean sage, bay and rosemary in winter, and basil and fresh tomatoes in summer (which for me means holidays in Provence). When you travel, eat the local food and register the defining spices and herbs, before bringing some back to scent your kitchen when you want to recreate the memory. For this effect you can use the real thing: fresh herbs and other aromatic ingredients in pots and bowls lend their own natural aromas to the room. An atomiser of an essential oil can top up the scent when desired, and can also be used to increase the 'productive' or 'organisational' requirements of a kitchen. For example, we know that mint and cinnamon enhance productivity and mental focus.

VANILLA, CARAMEL AND ALL THINGS NICE

Vanilla is a regular ingredient in perfume, but it also crosses over into an 'experiential' smell because we encounter it more often in food than in any other place. Along with other aromas like caramel, chocolate and strawberry, we associate it with indulgent food and therefore indulgent feelings. The scent of caramel or vanilla is as enticing as the sight of thick cream being drizzled onto a chocolate fondant. One study that sought to define the links between smell and touch showed that people relate sweet smells like vanilla to soft, smooth textures, and soft materials feel even softer when the smell of vanilla is in the air. In shopping environments, people move more slowly and buy more expensive items when the scent of vanilla or caramel is dispersed. Rich, indulgent smells also help give an atmosphere a slow, smooth, indulgent and luxurious tone. They would be perfect for the bedroom when you're doing more than just sleeping, or for a sitting room when the lights are low and you want to settle in for the night.

These ideas are just a starting point – there are many more options of 'experiential' scents that can be used to stir the emotions throughout the home, helping to define and enhance each room. Think about the smells and flavours that mean the most to you, and choose the ones that elicit the emotions you want to feel as you walk into each room.

Evoking nostalgic feelings is an enjoyable pastime on its own, and it's also really good for you. It has been shown to lower anxiety, make us feel more generous and open, and improve certain processes in the brain – and the latter is a key reason why it is increasingly used in the treatment of dementia and other degenerative diseases. At North Dakota State University, psychologists showed that people who had spent some time recalling nostalgic memories were more likely to agree with statements like 'life has a purpose' – a bit of remembering can be a life-affirming thing. A study in China revealed that warm memories can even actually warm you up. When people in a cool room were asked to reminisce about old memories, the ones who got really into it reported feeling warmer.

Slowing Down Time

The evening tends to disappear in a flash; you potter around doing a few things and before you know it, it's bedtime. It would be amazing if you could accomplish the impossible and make the evening seem longer – well, thanks to the world of sensory science, we have a solution. In the same way we had a sensory prescription for speeding up the end of the working day, it's possible to put one together that will slow your perception of time now.

FAST MUSIC
If slow music in a minor key makes time pass more quickly, it follows that fast music in a major key will make time pass more slowly, and research conducted in various conditions has shown this to be the case. One study proved that the

more uplifting and exciting a piece of music is, the slower time passes. At a laboratory in Bordeaux, participants were asked to sit in booths and rate different pieces of music as pleasant or unpleasant and calm or exciting, before estimating how long each track was. When the music was fast, people's estimations of the time that had passed went up; a minute felt like a minute and a half. But also, the more 'exciting' they said the music was, the slower they seemed to think time passed, so a minute might then feel like one minute forty-five seconds.

The researchers also reversed the music and played it to the subjects backwards, so that it wasn't recognisable or particularly pleasant, and the same effect was seen. The faster and more arousing the music was, the longer they thought it went on for. The pleasantness of the music was shown to not play a part in how it affects our time perception – it's all about how exciting it is.

AROUSING COLOURS – RED OR YELLOW

In the studies we discussed earlier that showed that the colour blue sped up the perception of time, the opposite effects were seen for the more arousing, warmer colours in the spectrum. In the experiment that asked people to judge the time a website took to download, time moved slowest for the participants when their screens were yellow. And if you want to push your arousal levels up a notch, red is consistently shown to be the most exciting, brain-stimulating colour. Both red and yellow are sensorially congruent to the upbeat music that you'll be playing, so place red or yellow objects around you when you are browsing online or pottering about. With the music pumping, you might feel like you've spent half an hour doing something, but only fifteen minutes or so will have passed.

BRIGHT LIGHT

Later on in the evening you should introduce a more relaxed lighting set-up to your home environment – having overhead lights on full blast doesn't bring out the best in anyone. Light that casts your eyes in shadow makes you look and feel tired and less attractive, while highlighting every foible in the room with stark lighting can make you self-conscious about your home and unable to relax. But at this point in the day, brighter light is better for inducing the state of alertness that will help slow down time. You don't want to undo all the calming and mood-changing that signalled your transition from work by recreating the strip lighting of an office, but you might consider turning the kitchen lights on or having a bright desk lamp next to you as you tend to your home business.

NO SCENT OR NASTY SMELLS!

The use of scent to slow down time becomes a tricky area, because studies consistently show that the presence of a pleasant scent makes time pass quicker. However, if you fill the room with an *un*pleasant smell, time slows right down. Researchers in France asked people to judge how long a burst of white noise went on for while they were sitting in booths. The participants were wearing dust masks, half of which had been imbued with decanoic acid, which has a rancid, sweaty odour. The poor people with the smelly masks, unsurprisingly, felt that time slowed down completely and the noise had gone on forever. The application of this is not particularly pleasant, but if you want to stretch out the evening, spray something nasty into the air – or if you have a teenage son, just sit in his bedroom and time will come to a halt.

A SENSORY PRESCRIPTION TO SLOW DOWN TIME

- **Music** – Fast and exciting. Play upbeat music with an uplifting feeling.
- **Colour** – Red or yellow – arousing colours that will make you more alert.
- **Light** – Bright – for this first part of the evening, turn the lights up to match the lively atmosphere.
- **Scent** – I doubt you'd want to do this, but bad smells slow down time. If your goal is to stretch out the evening, this is the moment when you should avoid lighting scented candles.

With banging techno and bright red lights, you might feel like you're in a brothel in Berlin. But if you follow the prescription and potter about, doing what you need to do, when you turn around to look at the clock, you'll be chuffed that not much time has passed.

There's still plenty of evening left; this is the point at which you can start enjoying the fun side of living a multisensory life. No matter what you're doing; any experience can be lifted by coordinating the senses. Coming up soon is a sensorial dinner that will bring everything together to create an immersive meal. But first I want to introduce a couple of other creative ideas that I hope you might find inspiring.

Immersive Cinema (Or a Box Set) at Home

The experience economy is booming – over the past ten years, everyone from chocolatiers to sports brands has tried to create immersive experiences for their customers. The mantra these days is PET – purpose, experience and talkability. This means having a brand purpose, creating an experience that encapsulates it for those who are lucky enough to attend and giving them stories to tell so they spread the word about the special memory they've been given.

Over the last decade, I have been involved in the creation of many of these immersive experiences. In order to make sure an experience truly embodies the brand's purpose, you must first look at the sensory science: what are the sounds, scents, tastes, colours, textures and behaviours that will convey the right message? Then you can use that as a sensory prescription from which to design your experience. When it is done properly, you will once again encounter this 'super-additive' effect, with everything working together to create a feeling that makes everything a better version of itself.

The explosion in popularity of these events is testament to how much people love them. Immersive dinners and cocktail experiences are everywhere (and we'll come to them in the next chapter), as are multisensory art installations and immersive theatre. The hugely popular Secret Cinema has gone from being part of an underground art scene to signing deals with the likes of Disney. At their events, theatre, fancy-dress, food, cocktails and cinema come together in huge, orchestrated moments of mass participation. Guests are taken on a rollercoaster ride of discovery, in a well-thought-out, detailed environment. They enjoy little moments of wonder, just as we do when we walk around a new town or city, but dialled up to eleven. Every moment becomes something to tell your friends, or perhaps the spark of an idea that might wean its way into your everyday life.

And so, as a starting point for recreational sensory living, why not create your own immersive cinema at home? There is scientific backing to the joys of such a practice; returning to the 'super-additive' effect, setting a congruent scene where everything makes sense makes every aspect of it more enjoyable. It doesn't mean going the whole hog every time – it's simply a matter of thinking about what you're going to watch in advance and then working out other sensory enhancements that could make the experience more enjoyable. Even on a weeknight, you can make a film more immersive and fun just by accompanying it with congruent food and drink. For instance, when I recently watched *The Avengers* with my son Linus, we made a spread of 'Tony Stark burgers' with 'Hulk sauce' (mayonnaise dyed green) and 'Captain America freedom fries'. We made all the lights in the room blue and red, Linus dressed up in a superhero costume (as he always does; master of enclothed cognition, that boy) and we played the film soundtrack while we were getting the food ready. Watching the film on TV suddenly became a special event.

Here are a couple of starters, using classic films as examples:

THE GREAT GATSBY
- Play a soundtrack of traditional jazz before the film begins.
- Serve vodka martinis or champagne.
- Make a platter of salmon blinis or another finger food.
- Spray some Tabac Blond by Caron perfume, the signature scent of roaring 1920s hedonism. The key ingredients, if you want to recreate it, are leather, iris, vetiver, ylang-ylang, cedar, patchouli, vanilla, ambergris and musk.

THE GODFATHER, GOODFELLAS OR OTHER MAFIA FILMS

- Play the theme from *The Godfather* or a playlist of Louis Prima, Frank Sinatra or any other 'mob' favourites.
- Make big bowls of sausage and tomato pasta (with the garlic in it sliced razor-thin).
- Drink lots of Nero d'Avola, a Sicilian red wine.
- Get some cannoli to eat later in the film.

PULP FICTION

- Put on the soundtrack to get yourself going before you start the film.
- Make Big Kahuna cheeseburgers with pineapple rings.
- Rustle up a '$5 milkshake' – the recipe is open to interpretation, but a splash of bourbon would be a good starting point.

A common pastime is to take on an epic box set, which is the ultimate time to set the scene and properly enter a world that you will be inhabiting for many hours.

DOWNTON ABBEY

- Lay your coffee table with a well-ironed white tablecloth, making sure you set out the cutlery with mathematical precision.
- Serve cocktails in teapots and teacups, or drink tea.
- Make some Edwardian canapés – oysters à la Russe,

cucumber sandwiches or Lady Mary's crab canapés.
- Scent the room with bergamot, a key ingredient in Earl Grey tea.

PEAKY BLINDERS
- Pour yourself a glass of stout or whisky.
- Spritz a smoky scent into the room.

GAME OF THRONES
- Pour beer (or mead, if you can get your hands on it) into oversized tankards.
- Serve a platter of bread, meat and cheese, cut into large chunks.

Sensory Travel Planning

Searching online for a holiday or planning activities for a trip sometimes begins with excitement but ends in frustration and decision fatigue. If you set a congruent sensory scene in the room first, your explorative sensation-seeking behaviour will emerge as your emotions come to the surface, making the whole process more fun.

Booking a beach holiday or some winter sun:
- Find a soundtrack of crashing waves and tropical birdsong to put on in the background.
- Choose some music that reminds you of your desired destination.
- Get out some sun cream and rub it into the back

of your hands, being careful not to get it on your laptop or iPad.

If you've decided on the destination but haven't yet booked the holiday, then buy some snacks or cook something from the region:

- Some olives and a plate of charcuterie if you're planning a trip to the Mediterranean.
- Summer rolls for a trip to Thailand.
- Tacos if you're off to South America.

If you're off for a weekend city break, then you can bring it to life in a similar way to build excitement:

- Researching restaurants to try in New York is more exciting if you're listening to Lou Reed, Jay-Z or Gershwin – depending on which side of New York you want to experience.
- Or you could do it while watching a classic New York film – *Manhattan*, *Working Girl*, *Taxi Driver* or many others.

Every moment of your time at home can be made more enjoyable if you take the time to set the scene and create a sensorially congruent atmosphere.

Now we've really got to the fun side of sensory experiences. The ultimate application of everything we've learned so far is coming next: sensory wining and dining. It's a part of life where all the senses come together, and a whole load of amazing new multisensory discoveries can help you create the ultimate dining experience. But first, a sensory sidestep to look into the realm of taste.

CHAPTER 10

Taste

Taste is a tough sense to isolate, because our perception of it has so much to do with other factors. Eating and drinking is a truly multisensory pursuit and our emotions and surroundings have a huge impact, as you'll remember from the Provençal rosé paradox in the Introduction. And as we'll discover in the next chapter, the sensation of taste can be manipulated by everything from the music we listen to, to the shape of the glass we drink from or the weight of the cutlery we use.

To start off with, taste and aroma are inextricably linked. Experts will argue that our perception of flavour is at least 80 per cent through smell – we all know this from trying to eat when we have a cold or holding our nose in order to swallow horrible medicine. I once used this idea to create an innovative way to taste Haig Club whisky (the one part-owned by David Beckham), in airports in places where you aren't allowed to hand out samples of alcohol. The United Arab Emirates, Vietnam and Singapore are all such 'dark markets', but they're also very lucrative for the whisky business. Given that tasting is the best way to recruit new buyers, my agency was challenged to devise a way to give people a taste of Haig Club without them actually *tasting* it. We turned to aroma, and by working with the master distillers, defined the exact flavour profile of the liquid before creating an aroma that smelled like the taste. It didn't smell like the whisky – if you pour out a dram and sniff it, you get a hit of alcohol, followed by the lighter and fresher notes. But on the palate it tastes sweet and it feels thick and viscous, with notes of banana bread and brioche. We created the smell of the taste of Haig Club, with the sweetness and viscosity dialled up to ten.

The aroma was then imbued into a blue ink, and a stamp was created of the Haig Club crest. For the 'tasting', a promotional person would stop a potential customer and say, 'Would you like to try Haig Club Whisky?' With the person's permission, they would stamp the blue scented crest onto the back of the person's hand. They would then ask them to raise their hand in a toast and draw it to their mouth as if taking a sip from a glass, breathing in through their nose as they did so. Inhaling the heady scent, the customer would get an experience of the taste that was as close as you could get without having it in your mouth.

There are millions of flavours, but only five tastes. For

a while there were just four – salt, sweet, sour and bitter – but then in 1908 umami came along, first identified by a Japanese chemistry professor called Kikunae Ikeda. A bit of an outsider, umami is a savoury quality that you get from ingredients such as mushrooms, tomatoes and fish sauce. The common belief is that these five tastes are all our tongues are geared up to detect, through taste receptors that sense amino acid compounds in foods and send information to the brain as to what we're consuming. They each have an evolutionary purpose – sweet to detect carbohydrates, salt to sense minerals, sour for acids, bitter for poisons and umami for protein – though arguments abound that there are actually more.

There is also spiciness, of course, but our perception of that is actually a form of pain. The key active compound in chillies is capsaicin, which triggers touch receptors on our tongue that act as molecular thermometers. They usually kick in when something is over a certain temperature, but because capsaicin lowers their threshold we experience the sensation of heat. Spiciness, therefore, doesn't particularly count as a taste – falling instead into the realms of touch.

A contender for a sixth taste could be a companion to umami called 'kokumi', which literally means 'mouthfulness' or 'heartiness'. The kokumi sensation is a widening and lengthening of flavours in the mouth; it is a taste enhancer that brings a depth to the other tastes. The issue here is whether we are trying to describe a taste or a sensation.

Kokumi was discovered in 1989 in the laboratories of Ajinomoto, the company originally founded by the umami pioneer Kikunae Ikeda. Flavourless amino-acid compounds extracted from garlic were added to other solutions, which suddenly took on a mouth-filling quality. The scientists started to isolate the types of amino acids that give certain foods that satisfying feeling, and the same compounds have since been found in cheeses like Parmesan and Gouda, as well as scallops, yeast extract, onions and beer. They are picked up on the tongue by the flavour receptors that sense umami and could have the same evolutionary purpose – to detect protein. This is why some people argue that kokumi should be classified as a taste.

In the same way that MSG (a synthesised version of pure umami) is used as a flavour enhancer in tinned goods and processed meats, as well as being added to low-salt foods to re-balance their flavour, kokumi could in the future be used to add that satisfying mouthfeel to products, or to enhance reduced fat foods. We've yet to see whether doing so will generate the same worries about potential health risks and artificiality, but for the budding chef, kokumi in its natural form is another useful weapon to have in the flavour arsenal. The idea is that you would be able to introduce hearty sensations to food by adding ingredients that are high in kokumi, in the same way that umami is now a consideration in the crafting of a good dish.

Metallic notes are another possible taste. We get the sensation when we taste blood, herbs like sage or stick our tongue on some metal. Having a metallic taste in your mouth can also be an early sign of pregnancy or the onset of medical conditions including kidney or liver problems, or even dementia. So we definitely can perceive the taste of metal, and you could argue that there's an evolutionary purpose to it if it's a signifier of so many bodily changes, but the question of whether it's a taste or not remains. No-one has managed to prove the existence of metallic-taste receptors on the tongue, as they have with the other flavours.

The taste of metal is an unmistakable sensation that has a kind of zing to it, and the theory holds that it is in part a form of electrical shock. Researchers at Cornell University have shown that a metallic sensation can be simulated by lightly electrocuting the tongue, just like when you put your tongue on one of those nine-volt batteries. In their experiment they showed that the simulated taste sensation was present when subjects held their nose, but when subjects tasted iron sulphate and held their nose, they couldn't taste it. This suggests that the true taste of metal is partly some sort of electrical stimulation of taste receptors on the tongue – a form of touch sensation – and partly a 'retro-nasal' flavour that is detected through aroma – so not a 'taste' as such.

Many other things that we taste may or may not be 'tastes'. It has been suggested that fattiness or creaminess is a taste, but it could just be a sensation that's linked to kokumi and umami. We are able to detect the flavour of calcium, and there would be an evolutionary reason to do so, as having it in our diet is important to our health. You can taste it in tap water and in foods like kale or spinach; the taste tends to be described as bitter, sour and chalky. Scientists have identified two calcium-tasting genes in mice, and theorise that they might find the same in humans.

If you really hate the flavour of bitter vegetables and have a dislike for overly fatty flavours, you may be what's called a 'supertaster'. All of us are either non-tasters, medium tasters or supertasters; being a supertaster doesn't mean you're super at tasting; it means you have a gene in your body that makes you sensitive to bitter and fatty flavours. Supertasters will generally be slightly thinner because they don't consume as much fat, and they can also be deficient in things like iron and calcium. To determine if you're a supertaster or not, there's a test you can take. All it entails is placing a thin strip of paper on the tongue, which is imbued with a harmless chemical called propylthiouracil. Non-tasters won't be able to taste anything and medium tasters will pick up something but won't react strongly. For supertasters, it will be disgusting, and almost unbearable. I've conducted en masse tests, and it's funny seeing a room full of people, with some of them blurting out sounds of disgust, while their friends are thinking, 'What are you going on about?' If you're not a supertaster, you won't get it. For those of you who have always hated brussels sprouts and spinach but have never understood why – maybe you were berated by your parents as a child – well, you're not fussy – you're probably a supertaster.

To add another complication, there is a difference between the 'sense' and the 'perception' of taste. What I've just discussed refers to what our tongues and noses can pick up, but our experience of taste is more influenced by our emotions and the other senses than any other. It's the reason why most of my work is with food and drink companies, from restaurants like The Fat Duck and food retailers like Marks & Spencer, to manufacturers of whisky, luxury chocolate and mass-market ice cream; considering every sense as part of the taste experience helps to enhance people's enjoyment and make the experience of eating and drinking more memorable.

Our sense of taste is a wondrous thing to explore as part of a multisensory life, because it's the place where all our senses and emotions cross over, giving you immediate confirmation that they're not separate, as we once thought. In a way, improving how we taste is the thing that I believe will change your life the most, as it did mine when I started immersing myself in this multisensory world. And so, without further ado, we will move on to the next chapter, to explore the wonders of multisensorial eating and drinking.

CHAPTER 11

Dinner and Drinks

Eating and drinking is the most multisensory activity we can indulge in. In my experience, if you ask a room of people what senses they use when they eat, all five may get a mention. They will, of course, say taste and smell. They will agree that we also eat with our eyes; beautiful-looking food begs temptation. They may acknowledge texture, considering how different foods feel in the mouth. And they may suggest sound, thinking about how they crunch or slurp their dinner, and the way that contributes to the experience. So there you go, all the main senses have been brought into the fold.

However, that answer would be only partly true; all these factors are a part of the experience of eating, but they are centred around the food itself – what it looks, smells, feels and sounds like when you eat it. What isn't being acknowledged is everything else around you. In order to acknowledge the full effect your senses have on your meal, you need to notice the colour of the plate, the tablecloth, the room and the lighting. The texture of the cutlery or your glass, the feel of the serviette and the comfort of your chair. The sound of the room, the music playing and the way the food you're eating is described. Stepping back further still, the entire atmosphere and how you are feeling at the time. All these elements play a huge part in our perception of how something tastes.

Food and drink are all about experience. Think back to the Provençal rosé paradox that began this journey, as we sat happily at an idyllic auberge with the sun shining down, a two-euro bottle of rosé tasting magical. If you think about the food you've enjoyed most in your life, there are a lot of emotional factors at play. Our favourite meals are often a moment in time when circumstances came together and created a perfect scene: a holiday meal at a beachfront shack; a family celebration with everyone sat around the table; an impromptu summer barbeque with a group of friends. In all these situations, location, emotions, company and flavours came together in the perfect sensory recipe for a happy memory. And as in the Provençal rosé paradox, we know that by creating an experience around a meal, engaging and indulging the senses in a congruent way, we can improve the taste of what we are eating or drinking.

The idea of 'dining experiences' is regarded as the domain of a handful of high-end restaurants, led by visionary chefs such as Heston Blumenthal, Grant Achatz and Paul Pairet, but it's something we can all enjoy at home. From choosing the right music to go with your wine to creating an immersive multisensory meal for a dinner party, it's all about understanding the sensory science of taste.

In order to delve into that wondrous world, let's imagine that friends are coming over for dinner and we're going all out to create an immersive dining experience that will tantalise their senses and leave them waxing lyrical about it for ever more.

The sensorial dinner party will play out like this:

1. Aroma Mixology: a sensory cocktail tasting
2. Starter
3. Main course: sensory settings to enhance the food
4. Between-course tongue twister: a colour-and-taste challenge
5. Dessert: amping up the indulgence
6. Digestif

Preparing the Meal – Some Considerations

There are a couple of elements to consider before your guests arrive. For this to be the best experience and for the food and drink to shine, you should pay careful attention to presentation and the atmosphere.

CUTLERY

An experiment was conducted in a restaurant: half of the diners were served their dinner with heavy banquet-style cutlery, and the other half were given lighter, cheap, canteen-style knives and forks. Everyone was presented with exactly the same food. The people who ate with the heavier cutlery believed their food was more artistic, they liked it more – it was reportedly around 11 per cent more delicious – and they were willing to pay about 14 per cent more for it.

ARTISTIC PRESENTATION

You may recall that when discussing the power of sight, I used the 'Taste of Kandinsky' study from the Crossmodal Research Laboratory in Oxford as an example of how presentation of food influences its taste. People said their meal was better quality and tastier when it was laid out in an artistic display. The study with the heavy cutlery mentioned above also included an experiment to see if presentation had an effect on the diners' ratings of their food, and showed once more that 'cheffy' presentation resulted in people liking the food more. We eat with our eyes, and the more creative flare you add to your presentation (without going over the top), the better – even if that simply means topping things off with a drizzle of oil and a sprinkle of herbs.

GUEST INVOLVEMENT

Depending on how Michelin-starred you want to go with your presentation, getting your guests involved at the table can range from letting everyone help themselves from a central platter, to giving each person a small jug of jus and instructing them to pour it artfully over the dish. Anything that involves your guests having a hand in the serving of the food will result in them liking it more – it's down to a phenomenon known as 'the Ikea effect'. The term was coined by the Harvard Business School professor Michael Norton in 2011, after a series of studies that assessed people's attachment to Ikea furniture, Lego buildings and pieces of origami that they had made themselves. Being personally involved in their creations and touching them as they were being made led to people valuing the objects more highly, aesthetically, emotionally and monetarily. When a group of people were asked to each build a mundane Ikea box, which was consequently put into an auction alongside other identical Ikea boxes that they hadn't built, they would inevitably bid for their own box, and they paid 38 per cent more on average than people who were just buying a box. When this was replicated with the origami pieces, the bids from the people who'd made the sculptures were nearly five times higher than those of other people, who regarded the pieces simply as amateurish and crumpled.

Following on from this insight, researchers in Switzerland proved that the Ikea effect can also apply to food – people's increased attachment to an item translates into them enjoying it more and consequently eating more of it. In their experiment people were asked to either taste a milkshake that had been made for them, or to make one on their own following a recipe they'd been given. When they made the milkshake themselves, they liked it more, rated it as tasting more natural, and guzzled down a significant amount more of it than those who were given one that was already made.

This might suggest that you should get your guests to make their own dinner, but their involvement in the creation of their food doesn't have to be total – just give them some active role and the Ikea effect kicks in. There's an interesting marketing story about instant cake mix from the 1950s that revolves around the same theory. When the product was first marketed, it completely failed. Housewives of the time felt no attachment to it – it made cooking too easy and they felt that it made their role obsolete. The product was consequently reintroduced to the market, but with a difference – this time you had to crack an egg into the mix first. It flew off the shelves – that simple act of involvement in the process had made the customer feel like the cakes that resulted were their own creation.

Your guests' involvement in the process can even be completely arbitrary. Back at Harvard Business School, Michael Norton was part of a team that asked a hundred or so students to perform arbitrary rituals, like banging on the table three times before tucking into a chocolate bar, and banging one time before eating some carrots. In each condition the students preferred the food, took longer savouring its taste and also ate more of it after they had performed the pointless ritual. Part of the effect was explained by the fact that anticipation had been increased when eating the food was delayed slightly by the ritual, but the students also felt like they were actively involving themselves in the process. The act of guests pouring the jus out or serving themselves from separate bowls at the table is similar. Or to really encourage the effect, give people a few processes to complete with some clear instructions. Your friends will feel more involved, more attached and will eat more food. And more importantly, they'll love it.

A WINE-LIST PLAYLIST – MATCHING MUSIC TO WINE

We're all privy to a food and wine pairing, so why not wine and music pairing? Listen to Blondie's 'Heart of Glass' and drink a Sauvignon Blanc and the wine will taste about 15 per cent more zingy and fresh. Why? Because the song feels zingy and fresh. Research shows that pairing the emotional feelings of music with tastes and flavours in food and drink enhances the taste in a congruent way. One of the most prolific researchers in this field is Adrian North, from the School of Life Sciences at Heriot-Watt University in Edinburgh. He showed that wine is consistently rated as tasting better when the music being listened to is 'emotionally congruent' – that means upbeat and light music for white, and dramatic or moody for red. One study asked people to rate the flavour of a Malbec, in silence; then they put on Carmina Burana by Carl Orff and tasted the wine again. With the music on, the participants rated the wine as tasting 15 per cent fuller and more robust.

A good way to experiment with this is to pour out a glass of both red and white wine and see which one you reach for when you play different music. Place the two glasses in front of you and put Blondie on (either in your mind, or preferably for real). Which one would you instinctively reach for? I'm pretty sure you would lean towards the chilled white. Now put on 'Bonnie and Clyde' by Serge Gainsbourg and Brigitte Bardot. Which one would make sense now? I'm hoping that this time you'd reach for the red. It should seem natural that different wine goes with different music, but it might be more of a revelation that the taste will actually be better when you get it right, or that it will be worse if you get it wrong. Never drink Malbec and listen to Debbie Harry – she'll bring out all the wine's tannins and the taste will be well off-balance.

For the perfect wine pairing, it's not just the emotional vibe of the music that counts; you can also match the instrumentation and other qualities. When you listen to 'Heart of Glass', that fresh and uplifting feeling comes through in every element of the track. The guitar is high-pitched, clean and plucky. The hi-hat is crisp and fresh. Debbie Harry's voice is high-pitched and glistening. The same goes for 'Bonnie and Clyde'. The sound is instantly lower-pitched, thicker and a bit rougher in texture. Gainsbourg's voice is bassy and gravelly, while Bardot's is low and smooth. Everything comes together to create a sound and an emotion that is completely in line with the flavour qualities of their corresponding wine.

Once you have this understanding, it's possible to put together a simple brief for the musical qualities that you should look for in order to match and improve whatever wine you're drinking. These briefs will work for food pairings as well, of course – the theory is the same.

Below is a brief for both light and full red and white wines, as well as a few musical examples to get you started. I've been as broad as I can with the music choice – it's simply a jumping-off point from which you can find songs that are more suited to your personal preferences. There are full suggested playlists for each wine type on the *Sense* website, too.

- **Light white** (Sauvignon Blanc, Albariño, Grüner Veltliner, Pinot Gris)
  Feeling – Upbeat, bright and happy.
  Sound – High-pitched, staccato rhythm, clean and crisp.
  Instruments to look out for – Plucky, stabby guitar.
  Tinkly, high-pitched bells. Crisp hi-hats and other percussion.
  Example tracks – 'Heart of Glass' by Blondie; 'Everywhere' by Fleetwood Mac; 'Love Is the Drug' by Roxy Music.
- **Full-bodied white** (Chardonnay, Viognier, Sémillon)
  Feeling – Mid-tempo, more contemplative than light white, but still positive.
  Sound – Softer, smoother and bright. Lush, full. High-

pitched and middle-pitched (still not bassy).
Instruments to look out for – Strings. Slow rhythm
guitar. Smooth synths. Soft backing vocals.
Example tracks – 'The Air that I Breathe' by The
Hollies; 'Mykonos' by Fleet Foxes; 'Cosmic Dancer' by
T. Rex.

- **Light red** (Gamay, Pinot Noir)
Feeling – Light. Cheerful. Mid to upbeat tempo.
Sound – Lower pitch. More bass. Less high-end
crispness. Staccato rhythm and a bit of texture.
Instruments to look out for – Plucky electric bass.
Plucky guitar. Soft rounded synths. Strings. Horns.
Example tracks – 'This Must Be the Place' by Talking
Heads; 'Do it Again' by Steely Dan; 'Cape Cod Kwassa
Kwassa' by Vampire Weekend.

- **Full-bodied red** (Cabernet Sauvignon, Malbec, Syrah,
Tempranillo, Bordeaux)
Feeling – Dramatic, bold, serious. A bit of attitude.
Sound – Low-pitched, full sound. Texture and
resonance. Mid to slow tempo.
Instruments to look out for – Bass. Low-pitched
vocals, with a bit of gravelly texture. Light distortion
on guitars. Acoustic guitar. Strings. Trombone.
Example tracks – 'Bonnie and Clyde' by Serge
Gainsbourg; 'Heartattack and Vine' by Tom Waits;
'(Wading Through) The Waters Of My Time' by Richard
Hawley.

A Sensorial Dinner Party

With the food prepped, the table laid and a playlist planned, it's time to start the dinner party. The following pages will take you through an evening of sensory surprises and discovery.

To kick things off we're going to have a multisensory cocktail experience, a great way to get the fun started and the senses tingling.

AROMA MIXOLOGY – A SENSORY COCKTAIL TASTING

The term 'aroma mixology' was something I came up with when I was developing some concepts for a whisky brand – I wanted to explore the world of cocktails, but didn't want to detract from the purity of the single malt that had been painstakingly crafted by the master distillers up in Speyside. By adding flavours in the form of aroma rather than putting liquids inside the glass, you can create cocktails without diluting the whisky, and the added bonus is that you can try lots of different 'aroma pairings' with one drink. It's really fun matching up different flavours and sometimes trying two or three aromas at a time, and as the opening part of a sensory dining experience, it gets people focusing on their senses and introduces a sense of play and exploration – as well as encouraging people to talk and interact as they try new combinations.

Firstly, make a drink This can be as simple as a G&T or vodka and tonic, or it works really well with a mixed drink that has a rich base spirit like aged rum or whisky, because of the more indulgent flavours that go well with them.

The best method is to put the scent on the back of the hand you drink with between the thumb and forefinger, so that when you lift the glass to your mouth you get exposed to the scent. As you take a sip of the drink, breathe in through your nose. The two taste sensations, one in your mouth and the other coming in through your nose, get mixed together in your mind, and you will taste them as one. An aroma cocktail! You can also put a different smell on each hand and switch between the two, enjoying two cocktails at once.

Lay out your ingredients You can create a really enticing display of aromatics and herbs at your table or kitchen counter, which will immediately get people excited and tantalise their senses. Lay them out in bowls so guests can explore picking them up, which will bring touch into the experience. Rub a bit of rosemary on the back of your hand – the smell will add a lovely tinge to your drink. Then layer it up, with some aniseed on top. After that you can all start to get involved, suggesting different combinations to each other. Here are some suggestions:

- Citrus peel – orange, lemon, lime or grapefruit
- Ginger

- Rosemary
- Fresh mint
- Coriander seeds or cardamom pods (both freshly crushed in a pestle and mortar)

For the 'experiential aroma' side of things, you don't have to stop at herbs and aromatic spices – you can use anything that comes to your imagination!

- Pine needles
- Flowers
- Freshly cut grass
- Pipe tobacco
- Pencil shavings

Or use essential oils This has a bit more of the feel of mad-scientist molecular gastronomy with the way it looks. Have a range of aromas in bottles, and get a load of scent strips (the kind you can get in a perfume shop) and dip a strip into each scent. Then hold the strip up to your nose as you sip the drink. The good bit about this method is being able to try several different scent strips at the same time and make crazy combinations. Grass, orange, vanilla and rum, anyone?

Now that everyone's senses are in sensation-seeking discovery mode, it's time to start the meal.

Starter

With each course of the meal, the aim is to change the sensory atmosphere in order to enhance the flavour of each dish, with an adjustment in the lighting tone and level, a spritz of an aroma over the table and some atmospheric sound. It's important to remember that the main event is still the food; the aim is to enhance the flavours rather than to overpower or distract from them.

It is not my place to say what you should cook, but for the purposes of this example, and to give inspiration for the type of sensory atmospheres you can create to accompany a dish, the starter is going to be something fresh and fishy.

Music-wise, you should have your light white wine playlist on. You can keep that going but add another soundscape over the top (maybe hide a Bluetooth speaker under the table) or switch entirely to the atmospheric side of things. Either way, it's time to recreate one part of a very famous dish from one of the best restaurants in the world.

A SEASIDE SOUNDSCAPE

At The Fat Duck, the three-Michelin-starred restaurant run by the innovative mad-scientist-cum-chef Heston Blumenthal, the whole meal is a journey of discovery. About an hour into this epic meal, you come to dish seven, which is possibly the most famous item on the menu: 'Sound of the Sea'. I had the pleasure of being involved in developing this amazingly inventive dish, by creating the soundscape that accompanies it. A beautiful glass plinth above a tiny sandpit is laid in front of you, topped with an arrangement of sashimi, tapioca 'sand', sea foam and pickled seaweeds. You are simultaneously presented with a large conch shell, with a pair of in-ear headphones popping out of it. Inside the conch shell is a mini iPod playing my soundscape of waves crashing and seagulls flying overhead. You are prompted to put on the headphones before eating the food, and you are instantly transported to the seaside. The combination of the sound and the taste is completely congruent, and the fish genuinely tastes fresher, fishier and more enjoyable. A few things are happening: the act of doing something unusual puts you in a state of unexpected expectation, where you're receptive to different things. The sound itself puts you in a happy mood – most of us will have positive memories associated with the sounds of crashing waves, and, as we have already seen, nostalgic memories have a positive emotional effect and open you up to sensation-seeking behaviour. Also, other sensory memories from being by the sea will be brought front of mind. You might recall the smells of the sea – the seaweed, wet sand and pebbles, the fresh sea air – and the feeling of sea spray on your face as the waves crash on the shore. Memories of eating freshly shucked oysters at a ramshackle beach hut may come flooding back. These sensory memories and emotions all combine to enhance your perception of the taste.

THE SCENT OF SEA AIR, OR AN AROMA FROM THE DISH

A spritz of scent from an atomiser over the table as you serve the plates adds a moment of wonder that should bring a smile to your guests' faces. If you can, try to get your hands on another common style of 'experiential aroma' that is usually called either 'ozone' or 'sea air', a perfumer's attempt to recreate that fresh, ozone, salt and algae scent you get standing on a pier or out at sea. If this isn't possible, choose something that is a constituent part of your dish – maybe water flavoured with a fresh herb like dill, or citrus.

LIGHTING

Brighter – you don't want to make everyone feel uncomfortable by putting the ceiling lights on full blast, but up the whiteness of the lights a bit, to enhance the fresh flavours and the seaside atmosphere.

Main Course

For this course, let's assume that you are having something nice and savoury – roast meat or a nice slow-roasted cauliflower, maybe with some foraged mushrooms.

AUTUMNAL FOREST SOUNDSCAPE

For such a dish, you could choose an autumnal forest or woodland atmosphere. The rustle of leaves blowing in the wind and scuttling along the floor. The creaking boughs of trees. The distant call of an owl and the tapping of a woodpecker. All this would go well with the umami earthiness of mushrooms and the woodiness and smokiness of roasted cauliflower or meat.

LOW LIGHTING OR CANDLES

Change the lighting before each course, but not only to enhance the taste of the dish – it's all about the experience, and a lighting change wakes everyone up to the fact that something is coming. It signals a moment, like turning the lights off before a birthday cake gets brought out, with all the candles lit. For this main course, light candles and dim the lights, making them a warmer orangey tone if possible.

SMOKY WOODFIRE SCENT

As a final sensory flourish, spritz a congruent aroma above the table to complete the scene before the food is brought out. I would choose a smoky scent to go with the sound, the low lighting and the candles; it would make you feel like you're in a log cabin up in the Blue Ridge Mountains.

The Between-Course Tongue Twister – A Colour and Taste Challenge

After the main course but before the dessert, I have an idea for an experiment that will tease your guests' taste buds, using colour to change their perception of flavour. The aim is to present your guests with two or three different-flavoured jellies, each dyed a 'wrong' colour (say, orange flavour, dyed purple), and ask them to try and guess the flavour. They will hopefully either taste something completely wrong or at least have real trouble trying to spot the taste.

This works because colour primes us to expect what we're about to taste so much that at times it can completely override what we're tasting. If the colour is incongruent with the flavour, we'll either taste what our mind thinks we should, like the wine experts being duped into thinking that white wine dyed red was actually red wine, or we'll taste something completely different. I once put on an event at the Westfield Shopping Centre in West London all about how easily our sense of taste is manipulated. In one room, we dyed a load of fruit juices different colours and tried to see if people could guess the flavours. Apple juice dyed red was most commonly believed to be cherry, and water dyed yellow was thought to taste of lemon. A similar study got children to taste normal vanilla ice cream, and when the same ice cream was dyed brown they all thought it was chocolate. In the same study the children were given unflavoured jelly that was coloured red and yellow – they said the red one tasted like strawberry and the yellow one tasted of lemon.

The tongue-twisting jelly challenge is pretty simple, and it's a molecular gastronomy-style interlude that will look very contemporary and might impress your friends.

1. Make two or three different-flavoured jellies
2. During the process, use flavourless food dye to make each one a colour that is incongruent to the flavour. For example:
   - Lemon flavour jelly, dyed red
   - Apple flavour jelly, dyed blue
   - Clementine flavour jelly, dyed green

   Or if you're adventurous, try the savoury angle:
   - Golden beetroot flavour jelly, with yellow dye added to increase the unexpected colour
   - Carrot flavour jelly dyed black
3. Set the jellies in low-sided trays, so you can cut identical-sized squares from each one.
4. Present them in a row to your guests on a long thin plate, having turned the lights up so the colours are easily discernible.
5. Ask your friends to identify the flavours as they go. The chances are that they'll get each flavour wrong.

Dessert

To finish the meal, we're going to use the sensory atmosphere to make an indulgent dessert even more indulgent. In this example, it's going to be a chocolate cheesecake with some fresh raspberries and a sweet raspberry compote. All the colours and cues for indulgence are there on the plate – it's just about dialling them up to eleven.

DEEP, RICH COLOUR

It is completely instinctual that deep, rich colour would be related to deep, rich flavours. If you were shopping for a punnet of strawberries, you would reach for the one containing lovely deep rich red berries over their slightly pale and pallid counterparts, knowing that they would taste best – richness and saturation of colour always communicate an increase in some quality such as flavour, strength or sweetness. And so the colours that surround this indulgent serve should all be deep and rich, whether a luscious red, a deep, enticing chocolate brown or creamy cream.

- Hand guests a warm, brightly coloured napkin to go alongside their dessert.
- Serve dessert on a dark-coloured plate – again red, brown or even black.
- Dim the lights or set them to a warm, amber glow.

ROUND SHAPES

As we've already seen, sweet flavours are associated with round, fluid shapes. Creaminess or sensual indulgence is too, so this is no time to serve your desert on a square plate or slate. But don't just stick to the plate; try to replicate the shapes elsewhere. You could choose an overtly rounded spoon, or make the food itself round instead of a triangular slice. A few years ago, confectioner Cadbury re-released their famous Dairy Milk bar with rounded sections rather than square; the company was instantly inundated with complaints about the change in the recipe and the added sweetness. But nothing had been altered other than the shape.

SMOOTH, SOFT MATERIALS

Everything your guests touch should mirror the mouthfeel of the rich dessert you're serving. Napkins should be made from a rich, shimmering, soft material that is silken or velvety in texture – the sensation directs the mind to similar sensations coming through the other senses. Consider the difference if you were holding a rough hessian napkin as you dived in. You might suddenly notice a slight grainy texture to the chocolate cheesecake. Keep everything as smooth and silky as you want the dessert to taste.

CHOCOLATE AROMA

As an extra flourish, spritz some chocolate aroma or light your vanilla candle from earlier. But remember not to do it too long before you bring out the food, or your guests will be sensorially satiated and may ask for a fruit salad instead. This is something to do at the moment they lift their heavy, round spoons to tuck in, raising the level of sensory indulgence.

SWEET MUSIC

The soundtrack for this moment can also emphasise the sweet flavours. I actually created a scientifically proven 'sweet' sound for a research paper, in collaboration with two chefs from The Fat Duck, Jocky Petrie and Stefan Cosser, and Charles Spence and Anne-Sylvie Crisinel from the Crossmodal Research Laboratory at Oxford University. The story of its creation marked my first foray into neuroscientific research. After creating the soundtrack for the Sound of the Sea, Jocky, Stefan and I were overcome with a desire to push the flavour-changing effect of sound and music even further.

I began by reading all the research that explored the crossover between sound and taste. The studies showed that there was a common thread to the types of sounds we associate with sweetness and the other basic tastes – sour, salt, bitter and umami. The methods of determining 'taste sounds' ranged from getting musicians to improvise after being asked to 'play something sweet', to sitting subjects in front of synthesiser keyboards asking them to find an area on the keyboard that they felt matched a particular flavour. All these studies had shown that people repeatedly place sweetness as high up and in a major key, with instruments like pianos and bells. Bitterness was always lower, with long, slow notes played on raspy instruments like trombones and bowed strings. What I also discovered on reading the research was that no one had tried it the other way around by writing a 'sweet' and a 'bitter' piece of music and seeing if they changed how those flavours tasted.

I took it upon myself to make two pieces of music that would change flavour, while Jocky and Stefan concocted some 'cinder toffee', a traditional English confection – sweet in taste but with burnt, bitter flavours too. We took both elements to Oxford's Crossmodal Research Laboratory, where Professor Spence set up an experiment to test our theory. Participants were sat in booths with headphones on, while a questionnaire asked them how bitter or sweet a taste was, where in the mouth they experienced the taste sensation and how much they liked it. When the experiment began, the participants were given a morsel of food to eat and had to fill out the questionnaire, while one of the sounds played through the headphones. Then the sound changed, and they were given a second morsel. Unbeknown to the participants, the food was the same both times – cinder toffee. But dependent on the sound, they rated it as tasting either really sweet or really bitter. The taste was at the front of their mouth with the sweet music playing and at the back when the bitter track was playing, and they liked it more when they were hearing the sweet sound.

The consequential paper, 'A Bittersweet Symphony: Modulating the Taste of Food by Changing the Sonic Properties of the Soundtrack Playing in the Background', was my first piece of published research. The sound is available on the *Sense* website; according to the paper, it will make food taste around 17 per cent sweeter on its own.

Digestif

Now the meal is done, and you should all be feeling well and truly spent, sensorially speaking. There is time for one final tipple, which gives me the opportunity to cover the sensation of touch and its influence on taste.

The shape and texture of anything you touch will steer your mind to seek out the corresponding flavours, making them appear more prominent. It's as if you're standing in front of a musical mixing desk of flavour, turning up the volume of some elements of the overall taste, so they become louder than the others in the mix.

The key is to identify the flavour that you want to dial up and to choose a corresponding texture or physical shape that will tune your senses into it. I recently applied this approach when I was designing the glass for a global beer brand to use in their Asian markets. Across the globe, we humans have different taste preferences that are, on the whole, consistent within individual cultures. People in Asian countries tend to like sweeter flavours and find bitterness a lot less palatable than, say, people from Eastern Europe. The biggest-selling whiskies in China and Taiwan, for instance, are the sweeter varieties. Vietnamese beers will be more sweet than bitter, while beer in the Czech Republic will be much more on the bitter side. The global beer brand that I worked with makes a beer that is well balanced, but definitely Western with regard to its flavour profile – it's lightly on the bitter side, and therefore not as appealing to Asian consumers as other lagers on the market. Using sensory science, I set a design brief for a rounder glass with a rounded texture on the front where you place your fingers as you pick it up, and a red dot on the bottom that would be in your field of vision as you drink. The glass tips the balance of flavour to the sweeter side; Asian drinkers prefer the taste, and the beer company doesn't have to spend millions creating a sweeter version of their beer recipe.

Depending on your digestif of choice and the preferences of your palate, you can select the perfect glass. The choice you have is whether to compliment or enhance certain flavours – you could take a bitter drink like a Negroni and serve it in a 'sweet glass' to level the taste, or you might choose a 'bitter glass' to accentuate it. The best way to discover what you like is to experiment. Pour your favourite after-dinner drink into a couple of different glasses, before tasting the difference and deciding which you prefer. From then on, you can have a special glass for that particular tipple. Here are some examples to get you started:

- **Sweetness, richness and viscosity** – A rounded glass with a satisfying weight and a smooth texture. A fluid shape and a rounded lip, so your mouth is in contact with the shape too.
- **Sourness** – Sharp, angular shapes and textures to focus you on citrus or sour flavours, bringing them to the fore. Angularity will also make drinks seem more refreshing.
- **Spice** – Rough, jagged, irregular textures will increase the punch of something like a spiced rum or a chilli-infused paloma. If you're drinking something bitter,

the roughness will accentuate its prominence on your palate, too.

- **Smoke and woodiness** – Glasses don't have to be made of glass. An earthenware or wooden cup with a rough texture will bring out woodiness and notes like smoke or hay. This is good for anything barrel-aged, too.
- **For a clean, clear taste** – A very pure and clean-shaped glass, with no texture and with little weight. This keeps the balance of what is in the glass as true to its original self as possible. It will enhance perceptions of purity and suit delicate flavours.

At the end of the day (which is where we now find ourselves), all these sensorial insights aren't just for this one big dining extravaganza – they can apply to every meal. To get the best out of everything you eat and drink, try to do a little something to set a congruent and conducive environment; and choose a fitting glass, cup, cutlery or plate for whatever you're serving.

We've been broadening our sensory world across all of our five senses so far, but it's time to go a little bit further and discover that there's more to our sensory world than you might have thought.

CHAPTER 12

The Other Senses

Throughout this book, we have seen the world through five senses: sight, hearing, smell, taste and touch. But it isn't quite as simple as that – in the same way that it's wrong to assume that each sense works separately from one another, the thought that human experience is made up of just these five is also a fallacy. Current thinking places the number of senses we actually have anywhere between nine and thirty-something, depending on how you look at it.

The classic five senses do make up the majority of our connection to our environment, which is why I've focused on them in this book. In order to live multisensorially we are mostly concerned with external stimuli – sounds, smells, colours, shapes, lighting, textures, weights and everything else that otherwise gets taken for granted or ignored. These are the elements of our sensory experience that can be controlled and coordinated to great effect.

But a lot of what we feel and know about ourselves and everything that's going on inside our body cannot be covered by the five Aristotelian senses. We have to look at our other internal sensory abilities, which are increasingly being acknowledged as our 'other' senses. Here are a few that you may be using right now, without even knowing it:

PROPRIOCEPTION

Close your eyes and hold your arm out. Now, with your eyes still closed, touch your nose. Did you find your nose? Good. You have just experienced proprioception in action. It's the ability to sense where your limbs are, described as a 'conscious or unconscious awareness of joint position'. It doesn't involve sight, smell, taste or sound, and it isn't touch *per se*; it's more than that. If you didn't have this ability, it would be hard to walk or to do pretty much anything. Our sense of proprioception is temporarily impaired when we're drunk – this is why we can't walk straight, and why the police might ask you to try and touch your nose in a drunk test. Athletes and sportspeople have a rather refined sense of proprioception because it helps with catching, kicking, hitting or anything that involves accurate motor control. For a sense that we don't particularly recognise, proprioception is fundamental to our lives; many people regard it as our sixth sense.

THE OTHER SENSES

BALANCE

Are you sitting upright? If you are, you must have a sense of balance, or equilibrioception – otherwise you'd be flopped out on the floor, feeling dizzy. We regularly refer to balance as a sense – as in 'that tightrope walker has got a great sense of balance' – but we don't tend to acknowledge it as a legitimate counterpart to the 'famous five'.

Our vestibular system, which is responsible for our sense of balance, is located in our inner ear, but it's not directly to do with hearing; after all, people who are deaf can still skateboard. It is only when the inner ear gets infected that our hearing and balance tend to go together. Sounds can throw you off balance, though; about one in a hundred people will at some point experience the 'Tullio phenomenon', which was discovered by the Italian biologist Pietro Tullio in 1929. When a sustained musical tone, like that made by a violin or trumpet, excites the vestibular system, your eyes roll as a reflex because the brain thinks your head is off-kilter. You then completely lose your sense of balance until the sound stops and the fluid that has flooded your inner ear recedes.

In this way, we can see that balance is very connected to vision as well. There does seem to be an order – your balance organs tell your eyes to adjust, and then your limbs compensate to keep you sturdy. This throws light on how our vision can trick us into being thrown off-balance when we watch a rollercoaster on a TV or stumble on the flat floor to correct ourselves while wearing a virtual reality headset. But our sense of balance is still switched on when we close our eyes, so it doesn't rely on vision. It's a separate sense with a separate system, but one that is influenced by and gets mixed up with the others – another player in our multisensory experience of the world.

KINESTHESIA

Have you ever been on a train sitting at a station, looking out of the window at another train on the opposite track, and sensed that you're moving forward, only to realise after a moment that it's in fact the other train pulling out in the opposite direction? That feeling happens because your vision has fooled your sense of kinesthesia, the ability to sense movement. Kinesthesia is similar to proprioception, but there's a difference: proprioception is knowing where your limbs are situated in 3D space, while kinesthesia is the awareness that they, and you, are in motion.

Professor Barry Smith, the philosopher and sensory expert who we've come across elsewhere in this book, has a great tale of when the cross-sensory effect goes the other way and kinesthesia conspires to change your vision. He says to imagine that you are sitting on a plane on the runway. If you look down the aisle towards the cockpit door, you can tell the plane is level – the door at the end is aligned with your eyes. Once the plane is taking off and you're heading up into the clouds, take another look down the aisle; you can clearly see that the door is above you and that the plane is now pointing up, but the view is exactly the same. In relation to where you're sitting and where the door at the end of the aisle is, it's at the same level to your eyes as it was when you were on the runway, but now it looks higher up. Why? Because your senses of kinesthesia and balance are telling you that you're hurtling upwards into the air; and your vision adjusts to confirm the situation.

INTEROCEPTION

Are you hungry? How do you know? Interoception, that's how! It's the awareness of internal sensations, such as feeling hungry, having butterflies in your stomach, knowing that you're going to be sick or that you need the toilet. The constant internal monitoring of receptors in your body keeps you up-to-date with these sensations, alerting you to anything that needs to be done to regulate your system.

Our sense of interoception forms a large part of our self-identity – knowing our own body and having the feeling that 'my body belongs to me' is central to our sense of self. It's something that as parents we should consider when talking to our children – as they are developing an understanding of who they are, they are constantly told that their interoception is wrong. They tell us that they're hungry and we tell them they're not. They say they they're tired and we tell them that they can't be. It must be very confusing.

This information can also be seen as fundamental to how we form and feel emotions, giving us what Antonio Damasio calls 'somatic markers', feelings that you link to an emotion which then become the signifiers of that emotion. You might feel a flutter as your heart rate speeds up when you're near a certain person, and because of your previous experience of what such feelings mean, you know you're in love.

That feeling and the flutter might then become linked to the person's smell, and so a bond can form between internal feelings, emotions and external sensory stimuli. The next time you smell that smell, it will trigger the flutter and awaken the emotion. Or maybe it triggers the emotion and that causes the flutter – the order of things can be argued either way, and perhaps it depends on the situation. But one thing is for sure – without interoception you wouldn't be able to feel the flutter of love in the first place.

MAGNETORECEPTION

Having a strong sense of direction could actually be a sense, too. Magnetoreception might sound like something out of X-Men, but it means being aware of the earth's geomagnetic field rather than being able to control metal objects with your mind. It's an ability that we know many other animals have – from birds that fly south for the winter, to mice, bats, toads and even certain molluscs – but it's always been assumed that the sense is missing from humans.

However, a recent study at the California Institute of Technology indicates that we do possess this ability. Subjects were sat inside a Faraday cage while a magnetic field moved around them and researchers measured their brain wave activity. They noticed 'specific and repeatable effects' on activity in the brain, which suggested the existence of an inbuilt biological ability to sense electromagnetic fields. The researchers suggested that we may have lost the conscious awareness of the ability over time. Despite this, most people will be able to think of a time when they've instinctively relied on their sense of direction, even if it was as simple as having a sense of which direction your hotel was in while walking around an unfamiliar city.

The list of potential senses can go on and on, depending on how granular you get and what you classify as a sense. Some people want to cut the existing sensory cake into more slices – does sensing temperature come under touch (as I have treated it in this book), or is thermoception an entirely different sense on its own? Some scientists would argue that sensing heat is one sense, and cold is another. One sense then quickly becomes three. Pain is also suggested to be a sense on its own – nociception – rather than part of touch. And there is argument to suggest that we can break sight down into a separate sense for colour and a sense for movement. If we follow this line of thinking, five senses can quickly become twenty or more.

The number starts to get really big when you broaden the definition of what a sense is. How about a sense of familiarity, a sense of humour, a sense of pride, a sense of justice and a sense of style – do they count? People can certainly have them to varying degrees, be naturally well endowed with them and lose them suddenly. There's the story of a person who lost their sight in an accident, and instead of their hearing becoming more acute they developed a strong sense of occasion. They couldn't see, but would always celebrate birthdays or anniversaries with a perfectly pitched level of enthusiasm.

Because of the various scientific and philosophical views, there is no one answer to the question of how many senses we have. But even if we keep to a reasonably rigid definition of what a sense is and bundle a few sensations up in one (heat, pain and touch together, for example), I think we can safely say there are at least seven and maybe as many as nine senses. No matter how many we decide that there are, the fundamental point is that none of our senses operate on their own. Loud music impairs your balance, and smells can make you hungry. I'm sure we could isolate an aroma that makes you feel like your arm is somewhere it isn't; or you could just have a few drinks. We are multisensory beings, however multi it gets; and the more we recognise this and tune into all the senses we use, the more aware of ourselves and our environment we become, and the better life gets.

CHAPTER 13

Sex

Everybody has now gone home, senses tingling, their hunger for experience and food truly satisfied. As you and your partner shuffle closer together, you both begin to think: 'Who's doing the washing up?' But then, once you have cleaned up the aromatics, herbs, scent atomisers and jelly moulds, and taken down the lighting rigs and hidden speakers, your minds might start to drift to the idea of intimacy. For if there is one thing that challenges eating for the most multisensory thing we do, it is sex.

I'm not regularly approached by clients with the challenge of using sensorial design to encourage sexual intimacy in their customers, but there was one instance when we were asked to enhance the build-up to and enjoyment of sex – we assisted in the development of a ground-breaking vibrator called MysteryVibe, which is now one of the top-selling products on the market. Its differentiating factor is its versatility – it can be manipulated into any shape, and it has six motors that can be independently controlled, for an infinite number of levels and types of stimulation. When I was brought in, the product was at prototype stage. My role was to provide design recommendations that would communicate and enhance feelings of intimacy, closeness and individuality at every point of contact with their customer, as well as the build-up of sexual anticipation.

Fluid, curved shapes ruled in the brand's graphic design. The sound used in their adverts and even the smartphone app that went with the MysteryVibe featured hushed whispers and delicate voices. Even the box emitted a soft 'shhh' as you slid it open. Soft, sweet scents were imbued into the packaging, and the vibrator was presented in a quilted pouch that doubled up as an eye mask. Every texture was soft but tactile, inviting touch and exploration.

The process that my team and I go through to deliver sensory enhancement is always similar. We begin by scouring the research journals to see what's already out there. Once we've uncovered insights into how we might communicate the 'key attributes' (which in the case of this project were intimacy, closeness, individuality and anticipation) through different senses, I find the connections that will be right for the product and the brand and identify the feelings and emotions that we want to evoke through every sensory interaction. The MysteryVibe project was a challenge, because the more you dig into the psychology and science of sex, the more difficult it is to pin down a set of absolutes. Taste, preferences and experience are supremely idiosyncratic, and all have sway over what turns us on.

However, there are certain sounds and aromas, colours and shapes that have the same physiological effects on us all – these are inescapable, irrespective of personal differences. The sensory signals we receive before and during sex are all connected to the original evolutionary purpose of making love. Beyond all the fun and enjoyment, we're still very primal creatures. Taking these signals and following the rules of sensorial congruency, we can put together a sensory prescription for sex that engages all the senses.

The Build-Up

Scent plays a huge part in how we appeal to our partners and can be the sole trigger for a night of fun and frolicking. Until recently, the role of smell in physical attraction was underrated, but over the years the evidence has stacked up, not least in support of the power of pheromones. These unconsciously detectable hormonal aroma molecules activate specific psychological and behavioural responses in other individuals. Their influence on attraction is triggered by an instinctual quest for genetic advantage, such as the desire to get busy with someone who has an opposing immune system, in order to produce children who will be less susceptible to disease.

A seminal study got women to wear T-shirts that had been worn by men with either matching or different immunological makeups; the women preferred the smell of the T-shirts from the men who were genetically different to them. Similarly, another study got men to look at pictures of women while they wore masks over their nose and mouths, half of which were imbued with androsterone, a postulated feminine hormone. The men with the scented masks said the women in the pictures were more attractive.

The theory exists that the act of kissing evolved because it gets our noses and tongues involved at the closest range possible, thus enabling us to smell and taste the compatibility of our potential mate. Kissing is all sensory – it involves touch, smell, taste and even sound, in the muted moans of agreement from both parties. At that most intimate moment, we give ourselves over to every sense, but smell is seemingly dominant at the moment of attraction.

BE NATURAL

The psychologist Rachel Herz of Brown University conducted a survey that sought to determine to what extent people acknowledge the importance of smell, and to see where the overlap is between a person's natural odour and an 'artificial odour', such as a perfume. She and her team developed what they called the 'Romantic Interests Survey', a set of eighteen questions that were posed to ninety-nine men and ninety-nine women on the Brown University campus. One part of the survey asked, 'If a potential lover was at least average when it comes to looks, voice, feel of their skin and their smell, which aspect would you most want to be better than average?' For women, the top two were smell and then looks; for men, looks were most important, followed by smell. Another section asked about the importance of a person's natural smell and their fragrance of choice when it came to being sexually interested in them. Results showed that both men and women would be most sexually attracted to a potential partner if they were clean and they liked the person's natural smell, and very uninterested if they were clean but they *didn't* like their natural scent. Liking their chosen fragrance was seen as attractive, but not as important as their natural odour. Overall smell was shown to be more important for women than for men, but still way up there for both.

According to this, we're much more attracted to a person's natural odour than to their artificial scent. If you're together, the chances are that you have an instinctual affinity for the smell of each other's skin. So the first rule for scent is: let nature rule. If you feel in need of a shower after this long day, don't apply artificial scents afterwards – keep your skin unadulterated.

LIGHT A WARM-SCENTED CANDLE

The smell of pumpkin pie increases the blood flow to a man's penis by 40 per cent. This was scientifically proven by a study that was conducted in Chicago, with the participants recruited through adverts on 'a classic rock radio station'. So there's your first caveat: pumpkin pie improves the erections of men who are into classic rock. In fact, every aroma used in the study, and they tried thirty combinations, increased the subjects' erections to some degree, and none had the opposite effect. Cranberry gave a 2 per cent improvement. The top scorer, pumpkin pie combined with lavender, showed a 40 per cent improvement, as mentioned. But the smell that came second, with a 31.5 per cent increase in blood flow, was doughnuts and liquorice. Third most effective was the combination of pumpkin pie and doughnuts. My second caveat is that this study seems to have been conducted exclusively on Homer Simpson.

The researchers theorise that the reason food-related smells have an effect on men's erections may be evolutionary – it was after our ancestors came back from hunting that they were more likely to get lucky. Or it could be linked to the state of mind nostalgia puts us in – sensation-seeking and open to experience. The most nostalgic aromas tend to be food-related. The smells mentioned seem to be culturally nostalgic to Americans, so maybe for British men it would be rhubarb crumble or strawberries and cream. I can only speak for myself.

We should take from these results that men respond physiologically and emotionally to enticing aromas, and the same can also be said for women. The key qualities of these baked desserts are warmth, spice and sweetness. Cinnamon, nutmeg, vanilla and anise are all key ingredients in the top three scents in the study. Lighting a sweet-scented candle creates a feeling of warmth on its own and the scent of these food-related ingredients will help things get underway – especially if someone has had one or two many drinks over dinner.

WEAR SOMETHING RED

In mating rituals throughout nature, many species perform some kind of display that involves the colour red, perhaps revealing the colour upon their plumage and ruffling it in the direction of a potential mate. Humans are no different, and researchers suggest that red is an inbuilt instigator of what they call 'reproduction-relevant behaviour'. A study in New York showed that during flirty conversation men asked women more intimate questions and sat closer to them when the women wore a red shirt than when they wore green or blue. Another study showed that women judged men in photos to be more attractive both when the men were wearing red and when they were standing against a red background.

This innate connection may partly explain the red light that Sting reassured Roxanne she needn't put on. And the attraction of red lipstick. The use of red across the ages to symbolise sex, lust and passion theoretically stems from this primal trigger.

ORANGE-RED LIGHTING

Although it does seem a bit obvious and potentially sleezy, going against Sting's pleas to Roxanne and putting the red light *on* appears to be both an evolutionary and socially learned turn-on. However, red lighting can feel too harsh and doesn't fit quite with the other sensory elements; a warm, orange-red colour is a gentler option that is also backed up by research. In 2016, the hotel chain Travelodge conducted a survey of over 2,000 British customers, asking them about their bedroom wall colours and sexual behaviours. The results showed that people who have caramel-coloured walls have sex most often, averaging around three and a half times a week (the UK national average is around twice a week). The researchers believe that it is because of a learned association between the colour and the pleasure of eating caramel and chocolate, and the link between chocolate and sex. A nice amber glow in the room is the nearest lighting can get to a sumptuous caramel shade and it also links sensorially to the warm scents of vanilla, nutmeg or pumpkin pie, with each element enhancing the presence of the other and creating an enveloping sensual atmosphere.

CURVED PATTERNS AND OBJECTS

Human beings, on the whole, prefer the appearance of curved, fluid lines, as opposed to straight and angular shapes. A fact that may be disputed by lovers of some modernist design, but none the less is confirmed by studies into the psychology of aesthetics – which suggest that our preference for curved contours is biologically determined because of our natural affinity to the human form. Back in 1947, the Cambridge psychologist Robert H. Thouless suggested that because curves are fundamental to the human body, sexual desires are at the root of our aesthetic appreciation of them. Curved shapes are also more pleasing to look at because of the smooth way the eyes move across an image or an object, as opposed to the staccato and abrupt sensation of following straight and broken lines.

As we've seen many times in our day, rounded shapes also relate to the naughty-but-nice elements of taste – sweetness, thickness, richness and indulgence. And it's possible that this link to sexual desire forms a part of that cross-sensory effect. In the world of product design and packaging, you will notice that the more pleasurable the product, the more fluid shapes are used in graphics, fonts, logos and packaging. When I've recommended the visual language of anything from a chocolate brand to the vibrator I worked on, the starting point of their design is always roundness and softness. Curved forms intrinsically cue up and enhance pleasure perception; they are also emotionally and sensorially warmer, which links with the scent, lighting and mood.

At this point in the evening, if you're choosing a bed throw, a blanket to lay on the floor or objects to decorate your bedroom, look for rounded contours in 3D shapes, and patterns with curved and fluid designs. This will create a more pleasing, rich and decadent environment.

MUSIC – LADIES' CHOICE

As you think about getting intimate, the background music is entirely down to personal choice. However, if you want some ideas, Professor Daniel Müllensiefen, a music psychologist at Goldsmiths University in London, ran a survey of 2,000 men and women in 2012, asking for their top musical choices before and during sex. Very unimaginatively, the favourite choice for men was 'Let's Get it On' by Marvin Gaye, while the top choice for women was the soundtrack to the film *Dirty Dancing*. It was also shown that men go to significantly more effort than women to choose music that might appeal to their partner, dramatically adjusting their musical preferences in order to please. Amazingly, both men and women in the study rated Queen's 'Bohemian Rhapsody' as *better* than sex – don't listen to that before you go into the bedroom, or it'll be downhill from then onwards, for both parties.

On analysing the musical choices in the survey, the consistent qualities of the tracks that get people in the mood were 'relaxed', 'tender', 'peaceful', 'happy' and 'low-key'.

During Sex

By 'during sex', I'm not just referring to penetrative sex, but the slow build-up of closeness and intimacy from even before the first touch, when expectation grows, the senses become heightened and the slightest touch or sound sends shivers across your skin. It is at this time that we should explore every sensation and revel in an intimate and shared multisensorial experience.

FOCUS ON YOUR SENSES

Be in the moment. Our minds can wander at the best of times, and there might be a temptation within some people to drift off and fantasise at the point of sexual intimacy. But research shows that being mentally present in the moment during sexual arousal can enhance the pleasure you receive from it. The whole concept of sensuality is defined by being fully absorbed in the experience of your senses. By using mindfulness techniques and focusing on the senses, you can keep yourself engaged. The more you connect with the touch, smell, sound and taste of your partner, the more present your mind will be.

TOUCH

The feel of skin is the most sexually stimulating texture on a physiological and emotional level; gently caressing each other releases oxytocin, 'the love hormone', which has a role in the prolificacy and enjoyment of orgasms, and in helping to forge the bonds of romantic attachment. Our oxytocin levels surge during the first six months of a relationship, but touching tends to drop off as time goes by. In an average relationship, men are the main touchers for the first year, after which women take over the role. The renowned sex therapist Linda De Villers is a huge exponent of what she calls 'non-goal-focused sensual touch'. She recommends spending some time stroking each other's arms and back, getting comfortable with being both a giver and receiver of touch, in order to forge deeper levels of connection.

CARESSING EXERCISES

Beyond our skin, the materials that cause sexual stimulation while touching or being touched are a matter of personal preference. De Villers suggests a multitextural exercise for couples to try out that can help you explore the textures and sensations that you do like. She suggests collecting up to ten different objects of varying materials, textures and temperatures: for instance, a fur mitt, a piece of satin ribbon, an ice cube, an emery board, a soft artist's paint brush and a toothbrush. Lie down naked and close your eyes, letting your partner (or yourself) stroke the side of your body and noting what you like or dislike, where you like it and the sensations that you're feeling. You may discover an entirely new sensory experience that you find enjoyable. De Villers suggests writing this all down as you go along, but I would suggest getting your phone out and using the voice recorder. Then you don't have to stop what you're doing to jot down a nice sensation, and you will also have a recording of the moments where texture caused a wave of sensual pleasure – a sexy sound that you can used to stimulate desire another time...

BREATHS AND WHISPERS

As senses heighten and intimacy grows, there's nothing closer and more personal than hushed, breathy voices. When Serge Gainsbourg asked Brigitte Bardot to make breathy sex noises in 'Je t'aime... moi non plus', the song was banned. Whispers are also intrinsically emotional, triggering memories of intimacy, care, attention and trust. Online there is the hugely popular and relatively newly named practice of ASMR, or 'autonomous sensory meridian response'. It refers to the effect of very close-up, delicate sounds and whispers that trigger a tingling feeling in the listener that begins at the top of the head and travels down the spine and throughout the body, causing feelings of euphoric relaxation. The term was coined by Jennifer Allen in 2009, after she discovered a community of people who professed to experience the same thing, and needed a scientific-sounding name for it. The effects have been under scientific scrutiny over recent years. One study got practitioners to watch videos while receiving fMRI scans, and the brain scans showed a response that is similar to the effects on animals when they're groomed. Activity was seen in the areas of the brain related to social cognition, self-awareness and social behaviours. There was also activity in the prefrontal cortex, which suggests the onset of oxytocin – this may contribute to the relaxing effect.

ASMR isn't a sexual practice, but the effects of euphoria and tingling are deeply pleasant, and it can add another level of sensorial intimacy to an already intimate moment between two people. Stimulating more oxytocin at the start of a sexual experience helps to strengthen a feeling of romantic bond – by gently talking or whispering to each other, you may not necessarily be stimulating an autonomous sensory response, but the act can be intimate and attentive none the less. To help create that sexy, close, personal mood, you could play music that includes breathy voices and hushed tones in addition to music that has ASMR triggers embedded into it to help cause the feeling.

MUSICAL 'SKIN ORGASMS'

There are other qualities of music that can add to the physical act of love, as well as heightening it emotionally. An effect sometimes referred to as 'skin orgasms' has been shown to be induced by musical passages that 'violate our expectations'. A study conducted in 1991 showed that around 80 per cent of subjects experienced shivers down the spine when listening to music that contained sudden changes in harmony, unexpected moments or places where there's an unusual discordance between two elements. Thirty-eight per cent of the people in the study connected the sensation to sexual arousal. Other studies have revealed that some subjects equate similar sensations like goosebumps or tingles down the arms to a form of sexual experience. Even if you don't feel the sensation as sexy on its own, it would be a nice extra dimension of sensation while in the throes of passion.

You might have been personally aware of this sensation before and know of certain songs or pieces of music that trigger the sensation for you. Even though it is brought on when there's an unexpected moment in the track, it works even when you know it's coming. Researchers in the field, like the psychologist Psyche Loui from Wesleyan University, say that the effect might be stronger when you're aware of it, as you will have built up an emotional memory between the song and the feeling.

Pieces of music that have been shown to generate skin orgasms include Rachmaninov's Piano Concerto No. 2 and 'Someone Like You' by Adele. I'm sure everyone will have their own favourites, but the presence of unexpected changes has been identified as one of the key triggers. Make a playlist of music that causes this sensation and put it on in the background, making your skin more sensitive while you focus on the intimacy of the moment.

SCENT TO THE MAX

People who have a more sensitive sense of smell tend to enjoy sex more, and women who have a better-than-average nose have been shown to have more orgasms. A group of researchers from Dresden ran a survey where they first assessed people's olfactory abilities using a method called 'Sniffin' Sticks', whereby the subjects sniffed scented sticks to see at what level they could pick up odours. Once the sensitivity of their nose had been established, the researchers asked the subjects questions about their sexual drive, desires and experience. The findings revealed a direct correlation between the people who had a better sense of smell and their self-reported enjoyment of sex.

In the same way that smell has an underlying primal influence in our attraction to other people, it also plays a huge part in the act of love-making. The researchers involved in the Dresden study talk about how our natural bodily smells, which are emitted during sex, are a significant factor in the experience. Therefore, at a time when the room is filling with sexy aromas, the people who have a heightened sense of smell are having more fun. As for the people who aren't as olfactorily endowed, it would make sense that the more you can smell, the better the sex – so amping up the aroma will engage your sense of smell and help you get more enjoyment from sex. The question then is what scents should we use? If we look to the world of aromatherapy, there are a couple of possibilities for what may work best:

Jasmine Jasmine has been used as an aphrodisiac in Asia for centuries, and there is a deeply rooted reason why it's a good option – it contains an aroma compound called 'indole'. This is a slightly off-smelling ingredient that is present in lots of things, like chocolate, poo and our own skin. Indole is released from around your private parts when you're sweating and because of friction, so it is effectively a major part of 'the smell of sex'. Having the scent of jasmine in the room could give you that extra hit of primal, sexy aroma that you might be missing out on if you don't have the most sensitive nose.

Ginger Ginger stimulates circulation, which could mean more sweat and pheromones. The Romans swore by it, with men chewing on raw ginger prior to a sexual encounter. It also goes well with the orangey-red glow of the lighting.

Amber Another time-honoured aphrodisiac, amber is a warm, woody, masculine scent. Researchers in Indiana showed that women enjoyed more intense sexual fantasies when they could smell a masculine fragrance. Amber has also been shown to increase blood circulation and therefore could get you hotter under the collar and promote the release of pheromones. Its colour also fits with the lighting element of our sensory prescription for sex.

Vanilla The scent is connected to sexual arousal in men and women, and it has been used as an aphrodisiac for centuries. In a book from the late 1800s called *King's American Dispensary*, it is purported to 'stimulate the sexual propensities' of those who imbibe its intoxicating aroma.

Sandalwood Another masculine scent, sandalwood is an aphrodisiac that was used in tantric sexual practices because of its supposed ability to heighten one's response to touch. In a study from 2006 that measured physiological responses to East Indian sandalwood, the essential oil was shown to elevate subjects' pulse rate and 'skin conductance level', which may explain why it has been favoured for so long.

With all these elements in place, we should have the perfect sensory prescription to have a very enjoyable time. Here is a summary of the facts:

A SENSORY PRESCRIPTION FOR BETTER SEX

- **Colour** – In the build-up, maybe wear something red.
- **Lighting** – Set the lights to a warm, orange-red glow.
- **Aroma** – Warm, spicy notes help on many levels. Get the room heavily scented.
- **Touch** – Caress each other's skin for deeper levels of connection. Try to experiment with objects of different textures and temperatures, to discover new pleasurable sensations.
- **Music** – Breathy vocals and emotive, spine-tingling moments.
- **Sound** – Whisper and gently talk to each other for closeness and skin-tingling sensations.
- **Shape** – Curved contours and fluid shapes in objects, patterns and designs around you.
- **Other** – Focus on the senses to bring you into the moment.

The Afterglow – Ready to Go Again

The days of the post-coital cigarette are long gone. In the era of the smoking ban, it's difficult to imagine anyone lighting up indoors, let alone in bed after love-making. And as for the idea of a post-sex 'vape', blowing plumes of synthetically sweetened mist into the air doesn't have quite the same cinematic feeling of cool to it. The idea behind having a cigarette after sex was that the smoke relaxes you and can potentially speed up the 'refractory period', the amount of time that it takes your body to recover after orgasm. In actual fact, ingesting nicotine has been shown to reduce a man's libido by around 23 per cent in the short term, immediately after a cigarette – lighting up seems like a sure-fire way of stubbing out any chances of another round.

If you're finished for the evening, most of the things that happen in your brain after sex are there to help you get a good night's sleep. After you orgasm, your body releases hormones such as prolactin, serotonin and more oxytocin, which all help you to relax and drift off. A study in 2012 scanned the brains of recently pleasured individuals and showed that the prefrontal cortex largely goes into shut down as well, reducing mental activity. This all adds up to the fact that you're ready for sleep, perhaps apart from sliding out of bed to clean your teeth. If that's the case, move on to the next chapter and see what can be done sensorially to help you on your way. If you want more action, read on. There are certain fundamental physical barriers to getting back on the horse, age being the main one. It's well known that the refractory period for men is longer than women. In a teenager it may be a few minutes;

over fifty, it could be up to twelve hours. Youth is wasted on the young.

For all those fifty-something men who are now vehemently defending their sexual prowess, yes, that may not be the case with you, Sir. A lot of factors other than age also come into play. The state of your relationship, the feelings of sexual attraction between you and your partner, your health and your libido can all drastically reduce that wait. And a few extra sensory additions can help, too.

SWITCH THE SCENT

The hormone prolactin that the body releases after we orgasm plays a large part in helping us drift off to sleep, but it also stimulates the brain to produce more neurons in the olfactory bulb, enhancing our sense of smell. Scent is a powerful motivator for sexual enjoyment, so this is a good time to stimulate your nose a bit more. The atmosphere will already be full of the smell of sex and the scented candle you've been burning, but now is the moment to change that aroma to something new, to counteract the fact that you may have got used to whatever you were smelling before. Smelling something new refreshes the senses and brings you more into the moment. So, after a few minutes holding each other and resting, get up and light an aroma that's different to what you had on before. Changing the tone awakens the senses and deepens the sensual atmosphere.

SEX

CHOCOLATE AND CREAM

If you're not too full after dinner or you're suddenly ravenous after sex, this would be a great time to get sexy with food. One of the problems in your body is a lack of the hormone dopamine, which gets you sexually excited, because other hormones in your body are suppressing it. Luckily, some of the sexiest foods, like chocolate, cream and strawberries, can increase your dopamine levels.

If you're in a new relationship, then your feelings towards each other will be further spurred on by eating something sweet. Scientists at Purdue University in Indiana showed that people who ate or drank something sugary rated potential partners as more attractive and were more interested in starting a long-term relationship with them. However, with couples who were already going steady, there was no increased attraction. The researchers put the effect down to what they call 'metaphorical thinking' – relating a sweet taste to having pleasurable feelings about someone and projecting them onto that person. In an established relationship, familiarity and experience will dominate over the immediate and short-lived effects of a sweet taste.

Introducing indulgent food into sex at an early stage in a relationship is a great idea. And if you've been together forever, the pleasure of eating something enjoyable is still there, so the rush of dopamine you receive will still have the same passion-inducing, sensation-seeking effect. If you choose this route, then in between love making you might 'do a Nigella', and pop down to the fridge in your dressing gown, bringing up a platter of indulgent food to play with.

PUT ON YOUR FAVOURITE TUNES

Listening to familiar music is another good way to increase dopamine release in your brain. One piece of research, conducted by Canadian neuroscientists, measured brain wave activity while subjects listened to music. They discovered two stages of dopamine release: one in the expectation of what is coming, and one in the experience of enjoying the track. When you listen to music that you know and love, you get a wave of dopamine as you sing along and a get another kick waiting for a part that you particularly like.

While you lie there together, eating and listening, everything should be conspiring to dissolve the tiredness and restore your libido, so you're ready for Round Two. And when you're finally done, you can begin your sensory run-up to sleep.

CHAPTER 14

Sleep

And so we come to the end of our multisensory day. If you've been following the routine down to a tee, you should be set up for a great night's sleep. If you woke up with light and the sound of birdsong, exercised at the right hour and spent at least a couple of hours in natural daylight, your circadian rhythm should be perfectly aligned and the balance of sleep-inducing hormones in your body should be just right. The importance of sleep on our mental and physical health cannot be underestimated – it's the bedrock of life, as vital as food and water. As the professor of neuroscience and psychology Matthew Walker writes in his book *Why We Sleep*, 'There is no tissue within the body and no process in the brain that is not enhanced by sleep, or demonstrably impaired when you don't get enough.'

Yet sleep is a big issue in modern life. Around 30 per cent of adults get less than six hours' sleep each night; fifty years ago, that figure was less than 3 per cent. As we learned in the early morning, our circadian rhythms are truly out of whack these days, due to demanding schedules, artificial light, computer screens and a lack of exposure to nature, as well as many other things that can get in the way of a good night's rest. We keep up bad habits that only serve to put our body clocks further off-kilter, but now's the time to stop. If we care about ourselves and our senses, we need a good night's rest.

This chapter does not claim to be a cure-all for the insomniac. For some people, it's a problem that requires specialist attention. However, there are certain sensorial considerations we can make that can have a hugely positive effect, and there are also some things we should avoid. The way to better sleep is in the ritual or routine that we follow in the run-up to bedtime. Starting two or three hours before, we need to stop bombarding our senses with the wrong kind of stimulation and to start treating them more thoughtfully. Envelope them in a warm blanket of multisensory bliss, so that not a single element is working against the goal. Try to calm, relax, slow and comfort, rather than counteracting our natural biological processes that keep us in sync with the cycle of night and day.

To that end, the perfect sensory prescription for sleep follows a countdown that leads to the moment when you close your eyes. All you have to do is work back from your desired bedtime and follow it as closely as possible. The first step is something that we should all know about by now, yet still fail to adhere to.

A Countdown to Bed

TWO TO THREE HOURS TO GO: STOP STARING AT SCREENS AND AVOID BRIGHT LIGHT

The LED lights that illuminate the screens of our smartphones, laptops and televisions are rich in the type of blue light that is shown to suppress the body's production of melatonin – the soporific hormone crucial for a good night's rest. According to the renowned sleep scientist Charles Czeisler of Harvard Medical School, staring at LED screens right before bedtime could be the most sleep-disruptive element of our evening routines. We should stop looking at screens at least two hours before bed, and preferably more like three. Televisions are less bad as we sit further away from them – it's phones, tablets and computers that are the biggest sleep-killers.

We evolved to sleep and wake with the natural cycles of day and night, but artificial light means that we no longer have to. Keeping ourselves up later with artificial light is disruptive to our circadian rhythm, but it's the presence of bright blue-white light in the evening that is most detrimental to our sleep. We are evolutionarily wired to wake up in the presence of that bright, blue-tinted light – dawn blue light is used in the cockpits of aeroplanes to counteract pilots' fatigue, and for some reason, most bathroom mirror lights have it pretty much spot-on, too. However, the last thing you should have in front of you while you clean your teeth before bed is a bright blue-white light. The bright spotlights that many houses have these days aren't much better. We can't go full blackout every evening, of course, but avoiding bright lighting can reduce the phase-shifting effect that night-time lighting has on our body clock.

A 2013 study from the School of Medicine at the University of Alabama looked at treating ADHD-related insomnia by suppressing the amount of blue light the subjects received during the evening. A group of adult sufferers all wore blue-light-blocking glasses between 8.30 and 11pm every night. Their sleep quality improved on multiple physiological measures, and they all reported feeling less anxious in the run-up to bedtime.

TWO HOURS TO GO: DIM LIGHTING WITH AN ORANGE HUE

One secret to getting our bodies back in sync is bright light in the morning and dim light in the evening. As you may remember from Chapter 1, light is the most powerful zeitgeber, or 'time giver', and can be used strategically to help align our natural rhythms. Scientists at the Lighting Research Center in Troy, New York, tested a treatment of light that involved one group of people being exposed to two hours of bright light in the morning and three hours of orange-tinted dim light in the evening, while another group received the treatment the other way around. After a week, the first group had advanced their 'circadian entrainment' by about two hours, meaning that they felt sleepy and were ready for bed two hours earlier than they had been before. The other group had pushed their body clocks back by about an hour, putting them even further out of phase.

By following our morning routine, you should get a blast of light as part of your alarm, and you'll hopefully have had a sufficient amount of bright daylight throughout the day. So in the run-up to bed, try to dim the lights and tint them orange if you can. The lighting in your bedroom should already be nice and low, but if you have nuanced control, turn down the arousing red tint from the love session and go for a softer orange. Otherwise, use warm bulbs and low lamp lighting.

FORTY-FIVE MINUTES TO GO: RELAXING MUSIC

One of my first jobs was composing music and creating sound beds for guided sleep meditations. The pursuit of the ultimate sleep-inducing music became an artistic endeavour, as I tried to identify the right level of melody, chord changes and general activity in the music that would be the perfect accompaniment to peaceful slumber. I would spend hours writing long, slow, drawn-out pieces of music and would then ask friends to try sleeping to them. The sleep meditations we created did very well and we received tons of positive feedback from listeners around the world.

Having background noise as you fall asleep and during the night can be helpful, especially if there is extraneous noise from traffic or nature outside your window. Sleep noise machines are increasingly popular, but it's in the run-up to sleep that music has the most beneficial effect. A study in Taiwan showed that listening to soft and slow music improved the sleep quality of older adults. A group of subjects aged between sixty and eighty-three were given a selection of relaxing music and told to listen to it for forty-five minutes before bedtime each night. They all experienced better-quality sleep, fell asleep more quickly and slept for longer. A similar study was conducted in Hungary, on university students, who were told to listen to relaxing classical music, an audio book, or silence for forty-five minutes before bed. Those in the classical music group got significantly better sleep and showed lower levels of stress and depression, but there was no difference between the audiobook and the silence conditions. So, listening to an audiobook isn't detrimental to sleep; but neither is it beneficial. Relaxing music is the thing.

The music you put on in the run-up to bed doesn't have to be the sort of soporific, sleep-inducing, ambient compositions that I used to make. Space out to a bit of ambient techno if that's your thing, but otherwise just put on some calm, soft and mellow music while you go through the last stages of the evening.

THIRTY MINUTES TO GO: LAVENDER AND CAMOMILE

The classic aromatherapy remedies for sleep show a positive effect in clinical trials. A blend of camomile and lavender used on patients suffering from insomnia on a hospital ward saw a 64 per cent reduction in the need for other forms of sedation. Another study showed that people who smelled lavender oil just before bed slept more deeply and had a greater amount of beneficial 'slow-wave sleep'. They also reported increased feelings of vigour the next morning, which the researchers put down to them having had a better night's rest. Interestingly, though, men and women seemed to be affected differently. Everyone slept better after the lavender was wafted their way, but it caused the women to have less REM and more light sleep, while men had more REM and less light sleep.

In both of these studies the people involved smelled the aroma before sleep rather than at the point they were drifting off, so try to introduce a lavender and camomile scent as part of your routine in the run-up to bed. Maybe apply a touch to your skin or bedclothes, so it's present as you potter about while getting ready for bed. Or scent whichever room you choose as the setting for your final restful activity before bed with a scented candle, atomiser or essential oil.

TWENTY MINUTES TO GO: RESTFUL ACTIVITIES

As a side-step from the sensory stimuli in your environment, it's worth covering a few recommended pre-bedtime behaviours that sleep therapists believe help calm your mind, lower anxiety and bring on drowsiness without stimulating unwanted hormones or brain wave activity that will counteract all your good work. Seeing as you're not watching TV at this point and have long put your phone away, you've got to do something else. With some relaxing tunes in the background, the lighting on low and a calming scent in the air, try to engage in at least one of these pre-bedtime practices:

Read Just six minutes of reading can reduce your stress levels and anxiety by up to 68 per cent, according to research conducted by scientists at Sussex University. The study began by increasing a group of subjects' stress levels through a series of tests and exercises, before they were asked to either have a cup of tea, go for a walk, listen to music or read a book. Reading was the most effective pursuit, and it only took around six minutes for the effects to kick in. Music was a close second, with a 61 per cent reduction in stress levels. The team of researchers, who were led by the neuropsychologist David Lewis, believe reading distracts the mind from feelings and thoughts that may be causing anxiety. The practice also eases tension and slows our breathing and heart rate, but make sure you're looking at a print book rather than an LED screen.

Write a list Writing in a journal for a few minutes before sleep has long been held as a worthwhile endeavour; the act of transcribing your thoughts gets them out of your head so they don't keep you awake at night. A recent study by psychologists in Texas and Atlanta sought to determine the best type of writing to engage in – planning for the next day with a to-do list, or recounting the day just gone. Fifty people were assigned a five-minute task to perform in the run-up to sleep: to write either a 'to-do' or a 'completed' list. Those who wrote the to-do list went to sleep faster than those who wrote a 'completed' list, and the more detailed people's to-do lists were, the quicker they fell asleep. Mapping out tasks and targets for the day or week ahead is a powerfully therapeutic act that alleviates anxieties and worries, allowing you to put your mind to rest.

Have a bath Other than being a relaxing thing in itself, there is a physiological reason why a bath helps you sleep. Counterintuitively, a hot bath cools down your skin, which then leads to longer and better periods of deep sleep. Our core body temperature drops at night, in line with our circadian rhythm, and is a marker that indicates when our bodies are ready for rest. After we bathe, our blood flow is closer to the skin, with its heat radiating into the air and cooling our core body temperature. We only have to lie in a hot bath for around ten minutes in order to reach the point at which this happens. Scientific advice would recommend that you bathe around ninety minutes before bed, but a quick soak at any time is still beneficial. It also provides an opportunity to listen to relaxing music and to indulge with a few drops of relaxing essential oil.

Meditate Several studies have shown the benefits that a few minutes of meditation can have on sleep. One study from the 1970s showed that chronic insomniacs who practised transcendental meditation before bed finally got to sleep, and that the effects continued in the long term. In a six-week trial in LA a few years ago, a group of adults who were suffering from insomnia practised mindfulness exercises in the run-up to sleep. They all showed significantly lower levels of anxiety, depression and stress and had longer and better rest than before. Mindfulness meditation involves focusing on your breathing and bringing your mind into the present, letting thoughts and emotions pass by without concern and clearing the hustle and bustle of thoughts and feelings. It is one of the many methods that we can use to induce the 'relaxation response', when our bodies undergo a deep physiological shift into a calmer state. With five or ten minutes of mindful breathing, the night should go more smoothly and you'll wake up feeling more rested.

A glass of warm milk Milk contains a sleep-inducing amino acid called tryptophan. Once ingested, it is converted into serotonin and melatonin, 'the sleep hormone'. Keeping a good level of tryptophan in your body is important regardless of sleep – studies have shown that people who suffer from stress and anxiety often have below-normal levels of tryptophan in their system. Once we top up our body's level, there is an almost instant feeling of calm and a lowering of stress, due to its role in serotonin production. It is present in high-protein foods like eggs, chicken, fish, some seeds and breakfast cereals. One study put a group of adults with sleep disorders on a diet of tryptophan-enriched cereals for breakfast and dinner. Their sleep quality improved – they slept for longer, moved around less in the night and felt less groggy in the morning.

You don't have to get your tryptophan hit from a glass of warm milk, of course. You could try to eat foods that are high in tryptophan all the time, but the idea behind the classic bedtime drink actually has scientific underpinning, as well as being warming and nicely comforting. Other bedtime drinks that are recommended by sleep therapists include camomile tea and banana tea, which is made by boiling a halved banana with the skin on for ten minutes in a pan and then adding honey. Both banana and honey contain tryptophan and help with melatonin production. A warm drink isn't a bedtime activity on its own, but it makes a good accompaniment to reading or list-writing.

FIVE MINUTES TO GO: TEMPERATURE

The temperature of your bedroom plays a large role in how you'll sleep. As mentioned above, your body temperature naturally cools at night, so being in a room that's too warm will counteract this, leading to disturbed sleep. The perfect room temperature for sleep is agreed to be between 16 and 19°C. That may seem a little cool for some, but at that level your body can maintain its optimal core temperature, enabling you to have a more effective and restorative night's rest. Just before you settle in, make sure the thermostat is set (if you can control it) to the optimal temperature.

AND SLEEP...

Close your eyes and drift off. If you've done everything through the day and followed a good bedtime routine, you should be in the land of nod in no time. Remember the power of a good routine is to do it as regularly as possible for the greatest effect. And going to bed as close to the same time as possible every night is one of the most important factors.

A SENSORY PRESCRIPTION FOR BETTER SLEEP

- Two to three hours to go – Stop staring at screens. Cut out all bright blue-white light.
- Two hours to go – Dim the lights. Warm orange glow.
- Ninety minutes to go – If you fancy a long bath, this is the perfect time.

- Forty-five minutes to go – Put on some soft, calm, relaxing music.
- Thirty minutes to go – Lavender and camomile aroma – on your skin, in a room or in the bath.
- Twenty minutes to go – A restful activity. Read, write, meditate, quick bath, accompanied by a warm drink.
- Five minutes to go – Make sure the night-time temperature won't be too warm. 16–19°C is the perfect range.
- Close your eyes...

While You Are Sleeping

But that's not everything – there are also some sensory elements that can be present *while* you sleep that will have a beneficial effect even if you are not aware of them at the time.

WHITE NOISE AND OCEAN WAVES

Many people use bedside sound machines to help them sleep throughout the night. They emit a selection of sounds that contain 'white noise' – a cross section of sonic frequencies that sounds like an out-of-tune radio. The sound is also sometimes a recording of the ocean, which sounds similar but in gentle waves. The use of these machines has been proven to be beneficial in hospital wards. A study in Tehran measured the sleep quality of critical care patients before and after the introduction of a white noise machine and found that sleep quality improved. A hospital ward in Huntsville, Alabama played ocean sounds and saw great improvements in the patients' quality of sleep. In a further study at a sleep laboratory at Brown University, researchers played a recording of an intensive care ward one night, with phones going off, conversation and sporadic activity, and then played the same recording the next night but with the addition of white noise. People slept much better when the white noise masked the recording of the hospital ward.

It's unexpected sounds that disturb our sleep or wake us up rather than the overall volume of our environment. When a constant blanket of sound covers the sudden spikes of noise throughout the night, we sleep more soundly. So if you have trouble with police sirens, animal noise or the cries of next door's baby, you may want to try – somewhat counterintuitively – increasing the sound level in your bedroom. A recording of white noise or ocean waves playing through bedside speakers will effectively drown out those other sounds; our ears adjust and set a new 'baseline level' of sound that then sits in the background while we sleep.

While we're in restful slumber, we might wonder what effect the sensory environment could still exert on us. We're improving our waking lives by being more multisensory, but can we do the same during sleep? The answer is yes. Firstly, you could have a bit of fun by sensorially guiding your dreams. And secondly, sleep can be a time when you can build upon the day's sensory prescriptions.

SENSORY DREAMS

When it comes to sound influencing our dreams, the person to turn to is Professor Richard Wiseman, creator of Dream:ON. By placing your smartphone next to you while you sleep, the app works out when you're dreaming and triggers a soundscape of your choice, such as a tropical beach, cityscape or woodland atmosphere. Wiseman's team ask users of the app to submit a dream diary – they analysed more than 13 million dream reports over two years, with fascinating results. It turned out that people's dreams are completely influenced by what they listen to. If you listen to a nature soundscape, your dreams will feature greenery, trees and flowers. You will dream about the sun when you have a beachside or even 'pool party' sound playing. Dreams that are accompanied by a natural soundscape tend to be more peaceful, while ones set to a cityscape are often more bizarre.

The same effect has been shown with aroma. Back in 1988, a pilot study tested a range of smells on people while they were in REM sleep, before waking them up and seeing if the smell had wormed its way into their unconscious mind. The success rate was around 20 per cent. One participant, who was wafted with the scent of lemon while asleep, recounted being in Golden Gate Park in San Francisco smelling the flowers, only they smelled like lemons – on some level, the aroma had clearly entered the sleeper's dreams. A later study tried to assess the emotional effect of pleasant or unpleasant smells; would a bad smell induce a bad dream, and a nice smell a nice one? The results showed a significant effect. The researchers exposed subjects to the smells of roses or rotten eggs, and those who smelled roses had more emotionally positive dreams.

The same team later tried priming the subjects, in order to link the smells with specific locations. Some participants looked at pictures of the countryside, accompanied by the smell of roses or rotten eggs, while others were shown images of a city while they being exposed to the two smells. Once the participants were asleep and dreaming, the smells were introduced; most subjects' dreams had a bucolic setting, while none dreamed of the city.

If we bring all that together, you might try to prime yourself for a location that has a strongly associated scent and sound – a summer meadow and freshly cut grass, or the beach and sun cream. Perhaps try looking at a picture before you go to sleep, with the sound and smell present, or you could set a sensory atmosphere of sound and aroma that fits the theme of the book that you're reading, like we did with films and TV shows earlier. Then as you sleep, when the two sensory stimuli get released, you should be transported to the scene. I'm sure this is technically possible, perhaps with a scent diffuser on a timer and a sound effect app like Dream:ON. Professor Wiseman suggests that the last dream you have before you wake up can affect your subsequent emotional state and behaviour; a sensory dream machine could be a way of setting yourself up for a good start to the day.

SLEEP CONDITIONING

A group from Harvard Business School have looked at what they call 'task reactivation' during sleep. It is possible to build upon the brain's natural night-time processes by introducing a sensory stimulus that was present during the day when you performed different activities. Along with behavioural scientists from the Netherlands, the Harvard team proved they could use this idea to enhance creative thinking. Before bedding down for the night, subjects were shown a video about a charity and given a challenge: as soon as they woke up the next day, they should come up with new ideas for how the charity might recruit volunteers. One group watched the film and pondered some thoughts with the smell of orange and vanilla in the air. During the night as they slept, the same aroma was piped in. The following day, the participants showed a significant improvement in their creative thinking and came up with more ideas than other control groups in the study. In a similar experiment in Germany, subjects performed memory tests with a scent in the room before they slept, and were consequently exposed to the same scent during sleep. When they repeated the tests the next morning, their recall had vastly improved.

These results are music to our multisensory ears, and the culmination of the day's practices – because if we use this idea of 'task reactivation' we can potentially build upon the effectiveness of the sensory prescriptions. We're already forging memories and associations, linking sounds and smells with specific tasks; reintroducing those elements in the night could help the brain process the information and condition us to behave accordingly when we hear and smell them the next day. For instance, working accurately on clerical tasks with the smell of cinnamon and the hubbub of a café during the day, we might have the same smell and soundscape present while we sleep. Our processing abilities would get a boost overnight, and then when a waft of cinnamon tea and the bustle of activity surrounded us at our desks the next day, we would be conditioned to be focused and productive. This might be applied to most of the things we've encountered throughout the day: thinking creatively with Play-Doh, making love with jasmine or tasting sweet flavours with tinkling bells. You would effectively be able to choose what you wanted to improve upon, and set a night-time training programme to reinforce connections.

In this way, the multisensory day never ends. The more we practise this sensorial approach to living, the stronger memories form and the more deep-rooted associations grow. We start to rewire ourselves in a multisensory way, using the sensory science to change our day-to-day performance and the pleasure we get from the finer things in life.

Acknowledgements

A special thank you to Jo for always believing in me. And to all my friends and colleagues at Sensory Experiences (formerly Condiment Junkie), especially Lindsey, Ioana and Lou.

Amassing this knowledge has been a wonderful journey of discovery for me that, in a way, began in the Experimental Kitchen at The Fat Duck many years ago – when I turned up armed with a load of ideas, and Jocky Petrie, Stefan Cosser and myself first started playing around with sound and food. Together we took our newly found enthusiasm to the strange underworld of the Crossmodal Research Laboratory at Oxford University, where Professor Charles Spence and his team rig up bizarre booths with out-of-date computers and Heath Robinson-style smell machines, discovering and uncovering this wonderful world of sensory synthesis. After publishing a few papers with the team there, I started broadening my scope from sound and taste to texture, colour, scent and beyond, bringing ideas back to Oxford, or to the hallowed halls of the Centre for the Study of the Senses in London, where Professor Barry Smith equally spends his time probing the extremities of the mind, investigating this strange crossing of our senses.

As I uncovered this world, I wanted to know more. And

with the help of some brave and open-minded individuals in positions of power at a few of the biggest brands in the world, I found an opportunity to bring together scientific study and artistic endeavour to indulge my hunger for innovation and information. I have been very lucky to have been paid to experiment and learn, and actually make things with my discoveries – building huge extravaganza events that tantalise the senses, or working with brilliant scientists to hone down the minutest nuance of shape, texture or sound that might spark a reaction and alter perception of a drink, shampoo or car. And so, to all those people I've worked with along the way, I thank you for the opportunities and look forward to many more sensory experiences together.

At some point in 2019 came the idea to write a book, taking my knowledge and experience and applying it to everyday life. I had always talked about putting pen to paper; I felt the time had come to give it a try. A huge thank you to my agent Jon Wood for taking a punt on me and seeing the potential for a book within my initial jumbled ramblings – and then pretty much coming up with the whole format and structure. Cheers Jon. And many thanks also to Wayne Davies for taking a leap of faith and signing me to your wonderful publishers. I hope it's worth it in the end.

I passionately believe in living more multisensorially. Engaging with our senses and our surroundings has the potential to make our whole lives richer. If this book helps even just a few people get more out of life, then it has served its purpose and I will be happy.